LOW-FAT
WAYS TO COOK
FAMILY
FAVORITES

LOW-FAT
WAYS TO COOK
FAMILY
FAVORITES

COMPILED AND EDITED BY
SUSAN M. MCINTOSH, M.S., R.D.

Copyright 1997 by Oxmoor House, Inc.
Book Division of Southern Progress Corporation
P.O. Box 2463, Birmingham, Alabama 35201

Library of Congress Catalog Number: 96-71086
ISBN: 0-8487-2215-9
Manufactured in the United States of America
First Printing 1997

Editor-in-Chief: Nancy Fitzpatrick Wyatt
Editorial Director, Special Interest Publications: Ann H. Harvey
Senior Foods Editor: Katherine M. Eakin
Senior Editor, Editorial Services: Olivia Kindig Wells
Art Director: James Boone

LOW-FAT WAYS TO COOK FAMILY FAVORITES

Menu and Recipe Consultant: Susan McEwen McIntosh, M.S., R.D.
Assistant Editor: Kelly Hooper Troiano
Associate Foods Editor: Anne Chappell Cain, M.S., M.P.H., R.D.
Copy Editor: Keri Bradford Anderson
Editorial Assistants: Meredith V. Mathis, Andrea L. Noble,
  Barzella Estle
Indexer: Mary Ann Laurens
Associate Art Director: Cynthia R. Cooper
Designer: Carol Damsky
Senior Photographer: Jim Bathie
Photographers: Howard L. Puckett, *Cooking Light* magazine;
  Ralph Anderson, Brit Huckabay; Randy Mayor (page 59);
  Tim Turner (page 131)
Senior Photo Stylist: Kay E. Clarke
Photo Stylists: Cindy Manning Barr, *Cooking Light* magazine;
  Virginia R. Cravens
Production Director: Phillip Lee
Associate Production Manager: Vanessa Cobbs Richardson
Production Assistant: Faye Porter Bonner

Our appreciation to the staff of *Cooking Light* magazine and to the Southern
Progress Corporation library staff for their contributions to this book.

Cover: *Pennsylvania Pot Roast (recipe on page 55)*
Frontispiece: *Spicy Joes (recipe on page 46)*

We're Here for You!

We at Oxmoor House are
dedicated to serving you with
reliable information that expands
your imagination and enriches your
life. We welcome your comments
and suggestions. Please write us at:

Oxmoor House, Inc.
Editor, *Low-Fat Ways
  To Cook Family Favorites*
2100 Lakeshore Drive
Birmingham, AL 35209

CONTENTS

MEALTIME MADE EASY

*H*ave you been looking for a way to prepare those luscious family favorites that you grew up with, such as buttermilk biscuits, meat loaf, and banana pudding, but without the extra fat, calories, and cholesterol? Well, fret no more! Low-fat ingredients and cooking techniques now make it possible to prepare healthy variations of these basic recipes that have been passed down for generations.

If you want your family to eat right for a lifetime, low-fat eating must become the norm—not just an occasional experiment. But you certainly don't want to give up your favorite foods forever.

Low-Fat Ways To Cook Family Favorites, a collection of recipes for basic dishes enjoyed by families across the country, helps you achieve a balance. The emphasis is on good food prepared the low-fat way.

Daytime Fare, beginning on page 33, features easy ideas for breakfast or lunch. The chapters following include recipes for main dishes, breads, side dishes, desserts, and even snacks. The primary criteria for selection were nutritive value, relative ease of preparation, and, of course, good taste.

But what about the finicky eater in your house? How do you encourage a four-year-old to eat what's good for him? On page 8, find strategies that have worked for other families, and discover tips on cooking for children throughout the book.

Most families today also face the challenge of time—there never seems to be enough of it. So before you start cooking, take a moment to review the following suggestions. These ideas can help you get in and out of the kitchen quickly, giving you more time to play with your kids, talk with your spouse, or just relax.

PLANNING AND SHOPPING

Before you enter the supermarket, take time to get organized. Plan menus, take stock of the pantry and refrigerator, and make a grocery list.

• Keep an ongoing grocery list, jotting down items as soon as your stock begins to run low.

• Plan weekly menus to include your family's favorite recipes as well as new ones you want to try. Write out your grocery list accordingly—organize the items as they appear in the supermarket.

• Plan ahead about how you'll use leftovers. For instance, after serving roasted chicken on Monday, use the leftovers to prepare a pot pie, chicken salad, soup, stir-fry dish, or tacos. Use leftover cooked pasta in soups, casseroles, or pasta salads.

• Keep on hand a supply of staple foods, like pasta, rice, potatoes, and pasta sauce. You'll be able to toss a meal together in no time with little planning.

• For a quick entrée, purchase pork, veal, or turkey cutlets; boneless, skinless chicken breasts or chicken tenders; or fish, shrimp, or scallops.

• Use canned fruits and vegetables for convenience. They also have optimal amounts of nutrients packed into every can.

COOKING AND FREEZING

With a bit of planning, you can minimize the time you spend preparing healthy family meals.

• It takes 8 to 10 minutes for your oven to preheat to the required temperature. Make preheating your first step in preparing any recipe that uses the oven. When preparing a meal with pasta, put the water on to boil as soon as you enter the kitchen.

• Thinner pieces of meat or chicken cook more quickly than thick pieces. To flatten meat or chicken, place it between two sheets of wax paper or heavy-duty plastic wrap, and pound it, using a meat mallet or rolling pin.

• For easy cleanup, coat grill racks and wire baskets with vegetable cooking spray, and line the bottoms of broiler pans with aluminum foil. Use a spray-on oven cleaner for hard-to-clean pots and pans.

• Make a huge pot of spaghetti sauce or chili; freeze it in small containers to use later for dishes like lasagna, manicotti, enchiladas, or nachos. Freeze single servings of soup or stew in individual microwave-safe containers for fast, help-yourself convenience.

• Freeze leftover pancakes or waffles. You can pop them in the toaster or microwave them to have a meal in minutes.

• When you have extra green peppers, chop and freeze them. There's no need to blanch them; simply place chopped peppers in a heavy-duty, zip-top freezer bag, press the bag flat, and freeze. You can also freeze onions, parsley, and cranberries.

Chop and freeze small quantities of fruits and vegetables for cooking convenience.

COOKING WITHOUT LOOKING

Don't let your slow cooker gather dust inside your kitchen cabinet. Use it to take control of your family meal preparation. Just put ingredients into the slow cooker in the morning, and turn it on. In the evening, supper will be ready when you are.

But how can you use the slow cooker for your own recipes?

• Almost everything, including vegetables, can go into the cooker at one time. However, add milk, yogurt, and sour cream during the last hour of cooking to prevent curdling.

• Add less water or liquid than the original recipe suggests since it will not cook away. You can always add more before serving.

• Cook noodles or pasta until slightly tender before adding to the cooker.

• Cook dried beans to soften them before adding them to the slow cooker.

• Keep the cooker covered during cooking.

COOKING TIME CONVERSIONS

Original Recipe	Low	High
15 to 30 minutes	4 to 6 hours	1½ to 2 hours
35 to 45 minutes	6 to 10 hours	3 to 4 hours
50 minutes to 3 hours	8 to 18 hours	4 to 6 hours

Note: Most uncooked meat and vegetable combinations will require at least 8 hours of cooking at low-heat setting.

KIDS IN THE KITCHEN

One of the best ways to give your children a positive attitude about food is to involve them in the preparation of family meals. If they have a say in what's for dinner and help with the cooking, they are less likely to turn up their noses at the table. Cooking together also gives you time to catch up on the day's happenings.

A child's natural development skills determine what tasks he or she can perform in the kitchen. Although kids mature at different rates, here are some general guidelines for food-related activities that you can expect youngsters to accomplish at different ages—all under adult supervision, of course.

Ages 4-6
• Gather ingredients and supplies.
• Add ingredients to a bowl, and stir.
• Roll dough, meatballs, peanut butter-cereal balls, and any other mixtures requiring shape.
• Peel bananas, hard-cooked eggs, and oranges.
• Wash fruits and vegetables; scrub with a brush.
• Tear salad greens, break broccoli and cauliflower into flowerets, and snap beans.
• Help set and clear the table.

Ages 6-8
• Beat with an egg beater.
• Fill up and level measuring spoons and cups.
• Hand-juice citrus fruits.
• Shuck corn.
• Peel carrots, using a vegetable peeler.
• Use a small, dull knife to help cut up semi-soft foods.
• Set and clear the table.

Ages 8-10
• Assist in making recipes that require only a few ingredients.
• Use a can opener.
• Use a microwave oven.

Ages 10-12
• Grate vegetables.
• Shred cheese.
• Use a conventional oven.
• Use a not-too-sharp kitchen knife.

Teenagers
• Plan menus and grocery lists.
• Prepare recipes with multiple ingredients.
• Work more independently in the kitchen.

Sneaky Strategies

To give your kids added fiber, less fat, and an extra shot of calcium and iron, try these quick tricks to boost nutrition without them knowing it.

• Substitute whole grains, oats, wheat germ, and unprocessed bran for a small part of the flour in recipes.
• Serve whole grain breads, bagels, and breadsticks.
• To provide more fiber, encourage children to eat fruit instead of drinking juice.
• Leave the skin on apples, pears, peaches, potatoes, and other fruits and vegetables. Be sure to scrub the fruit or vegetable thoroughly before cooking or eating.

• Substitute skim or nonfat milk, nonfat yogurt, nonfat or low-fat cottage cheese, and reduced-fat cheeses for high-fat dairy products in recipes.
• To increase the calcium intake, add several tablespoons of nonfat dry milk powder in addition to the liquid milk in blender drinks, muffins, homemade puddings, and pancake mix.
• Slip apricots, raisins, and prunes into snacks, entrées, baked goods, and desserts to increase fiber and iron intake. Also, add finely chopped cooked spinach or broccoli to chili, burritos, lasagna, or pizza.
• Make your own soft drinks from sparkling water and 100% fruit juice.

LOW-FAT BASICS

Whether you are trying to lose or maintain weight, low-fat eating makes good sense. Research studies show that decreasing your fat intake reduces risks of heart disease, diabetes, and some types of cancer. The goal recommended by major health groups is an intake of 30 percent or less of total daily calories from fat.

The *Low-Fat Ways To Cook* series helps you meet that goal. Each book gives you practical, delicious recipes with realistic advice about low-fat cooking and eating. The recipes are lower in total fat than traditional recipes, and most provide less than 30 percent of calories from fat and less than 10 percent from saturated fat.

If you have one high-fat item during a meal, you can balance it with low-fat choices for the rest of the day and still remain within the recommended percentage. For example, fat contributes 43 percent of the calories in the broccoli for the supper menu beginning on page 22. However, because the broccoli is served with other low-fat foods, the total menu provides only 26 percent of calories as fat.

The goal of fat reduction is not to eliminate fat entirely. In fact, some fat is needed to transport fat-soluble vitamins and maintain other body functions.

FIGURING THE FAT

The easiest way to achieve a diet with 30 percent or fewer of total calories from fat is to establish a daily "fat budget" based on the total number of calories you need each day. To estimate your daily calorie requirements, multiply your current weight by 15. Remember that this is only a rough guide because calorie requirements vary according to age, body size, and level of activity. To gain or lose 1 pound a week, add or subtract 500 calories a day. (A diet of fewer than 1,200 calories a day is not recommended unless medically supervised.)

To calculate your recommended fat allowance, multiply your daily calorie needs by .30 and divide by 9 (the number of calories in each gram of fat). Your daily fat gram intake should not exceed this number. For quick reference, see the Daily Fat Limits chart.

DAILY FAT LIMITS		
Calories Per Day	30 Percent of Calories	Grams of Fat
1,200	360	40
1,500	450	50
1,800	540	60
2,000	600	67
2,200	660	73
2,500	750	83
2,800	840	93

NUTRITIONAL ANALYSIS

Each recipe in *Low-Fat Ways To Cook Family Favorites* has been kitchen-tested by a staff of qualified home economists. In addition, registered dietitians have determined the nutrient information, using a computer system that analyzes every ingredient. These efforts ensure the success of each recipe and will help you fit these recipes into your own meal planning.

The nutrient grid that follows each recipe provides calories per serving and the percentage of calories from fat. Also, the grid lists the grams of total fat, saturated fat, protein, and carbohydrate, and the milligrams of cholesterol and sodium per serving. The nutrient values are as accurate as possible and are based on these assumptions.

• When the recipe calls for cooked pasta, rice, or noodles, we base the analysis on cooking without additional salt or fat.

• The calculations indicate that meat and poultry are trimmed of fat and skin before cooking.

• Only the amount of marinade absorbed by the food is calculated.

• Garnishes and other optional ingredients are not calculated.

• Some of the alcohol calories evaporate during heating, and only those remaining are calculated.

• When a range is given for an ingredient (3 to 3½ cups, for instance), we calculate the lesser amount.

• Fruits and vegetables listed in the ingredients are not peeled unless specified.

Pork and Pepper Skillet, Broccoli with Lemon, and Garlic Mashed Potatoes (menu on page 22)

SENSIBLE DINNERS

*Y*ou start your day early, as always. After a quick breakfast, you drop the kids off at school, and you stay on the run all day. Now it's time for supper—again! The following low-fat menus are guaranteed to provide you with the encouragement you need to prepare healthy, good-tasting meals for your family.

These include basic everyday foods that you can count on again and again. You may want to take a sandwich and fixings to the soccer field for a picnic. Other suppers include cheeseburgers, a skillet casserole, and oven-fried chicken. Rounding out this chapter is a meatless recipe for chili accompanied by corn muffins and slaw.

SIDELINE SOCCER SOCIAL

The next time your family heads to the soccer field, pack a portable supper guaranteed to fuel your team spirit. The Mock Muffuletta is a hand-held meal of roast beef, cheese, and salad. The flavors blend when it's wrapped tightly and chilled over crushed ice in a cooler. Serve Peanut Butter Snack Squares for a satisfying post-meal treat (analysis includes one per person).

Mock Muffuletta

Cheese- and Olive-Stuffed Celery

Peanut Butter Snack Squares

Flash Fruit Quencher

Serves 4
TOTAL CALORIES PER SERVING: 585
(CALORIES FROM FAT: 24%)

Mock Muffuletta, Cheese- and Olive-Stuffed Celery, Peanut Butter Snack Squares, and Flash Fruit Quencher

MOCK MUFFULETTA

3 cups finely shredded romaine lettuce
½ small purple onion, thinly sliced and
    separated into rings
¼ cup crumbled blue cheese
3 tablespoons commercial fat-free Italian
    dressing
1 tablespoon red wine vinegar
1 tablespoon water
4 (2-ounce) submarine rolls, split
2 plum tomatoes, thinly sliced
½ teaspoon coarsely ground pepper
6 ounces thinly sliced cooked roast beef

Combine first 6 ingredients in a bowl; toss well.
Spoon lettuce mixture onto bottom halves of rolls.
Top with tomato slices; sprinkle with pepper.
Arrange roast beef over tomato, and cover with roll
tops. Wrap in aluminum foil; chill at least 2 hours.
Yield: 4 servings.

PER SERVING: 294 CALORIES (27% FROM FAT)
FAT 8.9G (SATURATED FAT 3.0G)
PROTEIN 16.4G CARBOHYDRATE 37.4G
CHOLESTEROL 41MG SODIUM 781MG

CHEESE- AND OLIVE-STUFFED CELERY

¼ cup nonfat cream cheese, softened
1 tablespoon finely chopped green onions
1 teaspoon sesame seeds, toasted
4 pimiento-stuffed olives, finely chopped
24 (2-inch-long) celery sticks

Combine first 4 ingredients in a small bowl, stirring well. Spoon cream cheese mixture evenly into
12 celery sticks. Top with remaining 12 celery
sticks, pressing edges together. Cover and chill.
Yield: 4 servings.

PER SERVING: 27 CALORIES (20% FROM FAT)
FAT 0.6G (SATURATED FAT 0.1G)
PROTEIN 2.7G CARBOHYDRATE 2.7G
CHOLESTEROL 3MG SODIUM 339MG

PEANUT BUTTER SNACK SQUARES

⅓ cup reduced-calorie stick margarine,
    softened
¼ cup reduced-fat peanut butter spread
⅔ cup sugar
½ cup fat-free egg substitute
¾ cup all-purpose flour
½ teaspoon baking powder
⅛ teaspoon salt
½ cup finely chopped unsalted dry-roasted
    peanuts
½ teaspoon vanilla extract
Vegetable cooking spray

Beat margarine and peanut butter spread at
medium speed of an electric mixer until creamy;
gradually add sugar, beating well. Add egg substitute, and beat until well blended.
Combine flour, baking powder, and salt. Add to
margarine mixture, beating well. Stir in peanuts
and vanilla.
Spread mixture in an 8-inch square pan coated
with cooking spray. Bake at 350° for 25 minutes or
until lightly browned. Yield: 16 squares.

PER SQUARE: 126 CALORIES (44% FROM FAT)
FAT 6.2G (SATURATED FAT 0.9G)
PROTEIN 3.5G CARBOHYDRATE 15.6G
CHOLESTEROL 0MG SODIUM 84MG

FLASH FRUIT QUENCHER

2 cups cranberry juice cocktail, chilled
1 cup unsweetened pineapple juice, chilled
1 cup unsweetened orange juice, chilled

Combine all ingredients in a large pitcher, stirring well. Serve over crushed ice. Yield: 4 (1-cup)
servings.

PER SERVING: 138 CALORIES (1% FROM FAT)
FAT 0.2G (SATURATED FAT 0.0G)
PROTEIN 0.6G CARBOHYDRATE 34.6G
CHOLESTEROL 0MG SODIUM 6MG

BURGERS AND FRIES

Ask adults what they'd like for a special dinner and they might say steak with béarnaise sauce. But if you pose the same question to nine-year-olds, they're more likely to answer cheeseburger and fries. Before you head to the closest restaurant, try the burgers below. They're healthier, tastier, and even bigger than most fast food varieties. Top off the meal with refreshing Pineapple-Orange Frozen Yogurt (analysis includes ½ cup per person).

Mexican Chili-Cheese Burgers

Cheese Fries

Pineapple-Orange Frozen Yogurt

Serves 4
TOTAL CALORIES PER SERVING: 622
(CALORIES FROM FAT: 19%)

MEXICAN CHILI-CHEESE BURGERS

You may omit the jalapeño pepper for milder-flavored burgers.

1 pound ground round
1 cup seeded, chopped plum tomato
¼ cup minced fresh cilantro
1 tablespoon chili powder
2 teaspoons seeded, minced jalapeño pepper
½ teaspoon salt
½ teaspoon dried oregano
½ teaspoon ground cumin
¼ teaspoon pepper
Vegetable cooking spray
4 (¾-ounce) slices fat-free Cheddar cheese
¼ cup nonfat sour cream
4 (1½-ounce) hamburger buns
4 iceberg lettuce leaves
8 (¼-inch-thick) slices tomato
Grilled sliced onion (optional)

Combine first 9 ingredients; stir well. Divide mixture into 4 equal portions, shaping each into a ½-inch-thick patty.

Coat grill rack with cooking spray; place over medium-hot coals (350° to 400°). Place patties on rack; grill, covered, 6 minutes on each side or until done. Place 1 slice cheese on each patty; cover and grill 1 additional minute or until cheese melts.

Spread 1 tablespoon sour cream over top half of each bun. Place patties on bottoms of buns; top each with a lettuce leaf, 2 slices tomato, grilled onion (if desired), and bun top. Yield: 4 servings.

PER SERVING: 358 CALORIES (23% FROM FAT)
FAT 9.2G (SATURATED FAT 2.6G)
PROTEIN 36.2G   CARBOHYDRATE 30.6G
CHOLESTEROL 74MG   SODIUM 732MG

CHEESE FRIES

1½ pounds baking potatoes, peeled and cut
    into thin strips
1 tablespoon grated Parmesan cheese
1 tablespoon vegetable oil
¼ teaspoon salt
¼ teaspoon garlic powder
¼ teaspoon paprika
¼ teaspoon pepper

Combine all ingredients in a bowl, and toss well.
Arrange potato strips in a single layer on a baking
sheet. Bake at 450° for 35 minutes or until golden.
Yield: 4 servings.

PER SERVING: 200 CALORIES (18% FROM FAT)
FAT 4.0G (SATURATED FAT 0.9G)
PROTEIN 3.9G CARBOHYDRATE 37.0G
CHOLESTEROL 1MG SODIUM 178MG

Mexican Chili-Cheese Burger and Cheese Fries

PINEAPPLE-ORANGE FROZEN YOGURT

1 envelope unflavored gelatin
¼ cup cold water
2 (8-ounce) cartons plain nonfat yogurt
1 (8-ounce) can pineapple chunks in juice,
    drained
1 (6-ounce) can frozen orange juice
    concentrate, thawed and undiluted
¾ cup cold water
⅓ cup sugar

Sprinkle gelatin over ¼ cup cold water in a small
saucepan; let stand 1 minute. Cook over low heat,
stirring until gelatin dissolves, about 2 minutes.

Place gelatin mixture, yogurt, and remaining
ingredients in container of an electric blender;
cover and process until smooth, stopping once to
scrape down sides.

Pour mixture into freezer container of a 2-quart
hand-turned or electric freezer. Freeze according to
manufacturer's instructions. Pack freezer with additional ice and rock salt, and let stand 1 hour before
serving. Yield: 14 (½-cup) servings.

PER SERVING: 64 CALORIES (1% FROM FAT)
FAT 0.1G (SATURATED FAT 0.0G)
PROTEIN 2.6G CARBOHYDRATE 13.4G
CHOLESTEROL 1MG SODIUM 26MG

Fries without Fat

Bake fries instead of deep-frying them to
practically eliminate the oil. The key to getting crispy fries without the fat is to slice the
potatoes thinly.

Skillet Beef Casserole

COUNTRY COOKING

This hearty menu updates home-style cooking—you get old-time flavor without the traditional fat. The skillet casserole is full of chunks of lean beef, golden potatoes, and garden-fresh vegetables. An easy salad features the flavors of fresh spinach and red apples. And the new version of strawberry shortcake is sweet, delicious, and low in fat. Enjoy it with a cup of warm chocolate-flavored coffee.

Skillet Beef Casserole

Spinach-Apple Salad

Strawberry Shortcake à la Mode

Chocolate-Pecan Coffee

Serves 6
TOTAL CALORIES PER SERVING: 530
(CALORIES FROM FAT: 22%)

SKILLET BEEF CASSEROLE

2 (8-ounce) baking potatoes, peeled and cut into ⅛-inch slices
1 pound lean boneless beef sirloin steak
Vegetable cooking spray
½ cup thinly sliced carrot
1 cup thinly sliced onion
½ cup thinly sliced celery
2 cloves garlic, minced
2 tablespoons all-purpose flour
1 teaspoon coarsely ground pepper
¾ teaspoon dried whole thyme
1 (16-ounce) can no-salt-added green beans, drained
1 (14½-ounce) can no-salt-added whole tomatoes, drained and chopped
1 (5½-ounce) can no-salt-added vegetable juice
2 teaspoons reduced-calorie margarine, melted

Cook potato slices in boiling water to cover 3 minutes or until crisp-tender. Drain and set aside.

Trim fat from steak; cut steak into 1-inch pieces. Coat a 10-inch ovenproof skillet with cooking spray; place over medium-high heat until hot. Add steak; cook until browned on all sides, turning occasionally. Remove from skillet, and set aside. Wipe drippings from skillet with a paper towel.

Coat skillet with cooking spray. Add carrot; sauté 4 to 5 minutes. Add onion, celery, and garlic, and sauté until vegetables are tender.

Combine flour, pepper, and thyme; stir mixture well. Stir flour mixture into vegetable mixture; cook, stirring constantly, 1 minute. Add beef, green beans, tomatoes, and vegetable juice. Bring to a boil; reduce heat, and simmer 5 minutes, stirring occasionally.

Remove skillet from heat; arrange potato slices over beef mixture to cover completely. Brush potato with margarine. Broil 5½ inches from heat (with electric oven door partially opened) 15 minutes or until golden. Yield: 6 servings.

PER SERVING: 197 CALORIES (25% FROM FAT)
FAT 5.5G (SATURATED FAT 1.9G)
PROTEIN 18.4G CARBOHYDRATE 19.2G
CHOLESTEROL 43MG SODIUM 77MG

Spinach-Apple Salad

6 cups torn fresh spinach
½ cup chopped Red Delicious apple
¼ cup golden raisins
2 tablespoons slivered almonds, toasted
¼ cup plus 1 tablespoon unsweetened apple
    juice
3 tablespoons cider vinegar
1 teaspoon Dijon mustard
1 teaspoon vegetable oil
¼ teaspoon garlic powder
¼ teaspoon pepper

Combine first 4 ingredients in a large bowl, and toss gently.

Combine apple juice and remaining 5 ingredients in a small jar; cover tightly, and shake vigorously. Pour over spinach mixture, and toss gently. Yield: 6 (1-cup) servings.

Per Serving: 61 Calories (30% from Fat)
Fat 2.0g (Saturated Fat 0.3g)
Protein 1.5g Carbohydrate 10.8g
Cholesterol 0mg Sodium 49mg

Strawberry Shortcake à la Mode

3 cups fresh strawberries, sliced
2 tablespoons sugar
1¾ cups plus 2 teaspoons all-purpose flour,
    divided
2 teaspoons baking powder
¼ teaspoon baking soda
¼ teaspoon salt
2 teaspoons sugar
3 tablespoons reduced-calorie stick margarine
½ cup plus 2 tablespoons plain nonfat yogurt
¾ cup vanilla low-fat ice cream, softened

Combine strawberry slices and 2 tablespoons sugar in a medium bowl; stir gently. Cover and chill at least 45 minutes.

Combine 1¾ cups flour and next 4 ingredients in a bowl; cut in margarine with a pastry blender until mixture resembles coarse meal. Add yogurt, stirring just until dry ingredients are moistened.

Sprinkle remaining 2 teaspoons flour evenly over work surface. Turn dough out onto floured surface, and knead 4 or 5 times.

Roll dough to ⅝-inch thickness; cut dough into 6 rounds with a 3-inch biscuit cutter. Place rounds on an ungreased baking sheet. Bake at 425° for 8 to 10 minutes or until biscuits are golden. Remove from baking sheet, and cool on a wire rack.

Cut each biscuit in half horizontally; place each bottom half on an individual dessert plate. Spoon half of strawberry mixture evenly over bottom halves of biscuits; cover with tops of biscuits. Top evenly with remaining strawberry mixture. Spoon 2 tablespoons ice cream over each serving; serve immediately. Yield: 6 servings.

Per Serving: 240 Calories (20% from Fat)
Fat 5.3g (Saturated Fat 1.2g)
Protein 5.9g Carbohydrate 43.0g
Cholesterol 4mg Sodium 318mg

Chocolate-Pecan Coffee

½ cup medium-grind pecan-flavored
    coffee granules
1 tablespoon unsweetened cocoa
½ teaspoon ground cinnamon
5 cups water
3 tablespoons chocolate-flavored syrup

Combine first 3 ingredients in basket of a drip coffeemaker or electric percolator. Place water in pot. Prepare coffee according to manufacturer's instructions. Stir in chocolate syrup, and serve immediately. Yield: 6 (¾-cup) servings.

Per Serving: 32 Calories (8% from Fat)
Fat 0.3g (Saturated Fat 0.1g)
Protein 0.7g Carbohydrate 6.8g
Cholesterol 0mg Sodium 10mg

DOWN-HOME DINNER

Try serving this Southern-inspired menu on the porch, and invite the neighbors for dinner. Start by making the ice cream mixture for the dessert. While the beans and rice simmer, prepare the greens and assemble the salad. Add orange slices to the dinner plate for a colorful garnish. Cook the peaches, and top them with the cinnamon ice cream just before serving.

Red Beans and Rice

Braised Greens

Watermelon with Celery Dressing

Spiced Peaches with Cinnamon Ice Cream

Serves 6
TOTAL CALORIES PER SERVING: 512
(CALORIES FROM FAT: 22%)

RED BEANS AND RICE

*Beans are low in fat, high in fiber and protein, and packed
with vitamins and minerals—all good reasons to eat them often.*

Vegetable cooking spray
2 teaspoons olive oil
1 cup chopped onion
1½ cups instant rice, uncooked
¼ teaspoon ground red pepper
⅛ teaspoon paprika
3 bay leaves
2 (15-ounce) cans red kidney beans, rinsed
and drained
2 (14¼-ounce) cans no-salt-added beef broth
1 (6-ounce) package sliced Canadian bacon,
coarsely chopped
1 cup seeded, chopped tomato
3 tablespoons sliced green onions

Coat a Dutch oven with cooking spray; add oil. Place over medium-high heat until hot. Add onion; sauté until tender.

Add rice and next 6 ingredients. Bring mixture to a boil; cover, reduce heat, and simmer 15 minutes or until liquid is absorbed and rice is tender. Remove and discard bay leaves.

To serve, ladle into six individual bowls, and top evenly with tomato and green onions. Yield: 6 (1⅓-cup) servings.

PER SERVING: 247 CALORIES (16% FROM FAT)
FAT 4.3G (SATURATED FAT 0.9G)
PROTEIN 12.8G   CARBOHYDRATE 37.5G
CHOLESTEROL 14MG   SODIUM 688MG

Red Beans and Rice, Braised Greens, and Watermelon with Celery Dressing

BRAISED GREENS

1 pound fresh turnip greens
Vegetable cooking spray
1 teaspoon vegetable oil
¼ cup diced onion
1 tablespoon balsamic vinegar
1 teaspoon sugar
¼ teaspoon dried crushed red pepper

Remove and discard tough stems from greens; wash greens thoroughly. Drain (do not pat dry). Place greens in a Dutch oven (do not add water). Cover and cook over medium heat 8 to 10 minutes or until tender. Drain well, and pat dry with paper towels. Coarsely chop greens, and set aside.

Coat a large nonstick skillet with cooking spray, and add oil. Place over medium-high heat until hot. Add diced onion, and sauté 2 to 3 minutes or until tender. Add greens, vinegar, sugar, and pepper; stir well. Cook, uncovered, 5 minutes or until thoroughly heated, stirring often. Yield: 6 (½-cup) servings.

PER SERVING: 32 CALORIES (34% FROM FAT)
FAT 1.2G (SATURATED FAT 0.2G)
PROTEIN 1.1G CARBOHYDRATE 5.2G
CHOLESTEROL 0MG SODIUM 27MG

WATERMELON WITH CELERY DRESSING

¼ cup low-fat sour cream
¼ cup plain nonfat yogurt
2 tablespoons skim milk
½ cup finely chopped celery
6 cups seeded, cubed watermelon
6 green leaf lettuce leaves

Combine first 3 ingredients in a bowl; stir until smooth. Add celery; stir well. Place 1 cup watermelon on each of six lettuce-lined salad plates, and top evenly with dressing. Yield: 6 servings.

PER SERVING: 76 CALORIES (24% FROM FAT)
FAT 2.0G (SATURATED FAT 1.1G)
PROTEIN 2.3G CARBOHYDRATE 13.6G
CHOLESTEROL 4MG SODIUM 28MG

SPICED PEACHES WITH CINNAMON ICE CREAM

1¾ cups vanilla low-fat ice cream, softened
1 teaspoon ground cinnamon
¼ cup firmly packed brown sugar
2 tablespoons unsweetened apple juice
1½ tablespoons reduced-calorie margarine
1 teaspoon lemon juice
¼ teaspoon ground allspice
3 cups frozen sliced peaches, thawed
2 tablespoons chopped pecans, toasted

Combine ice cream and cinnamon in a medium bowl, stirring well. Cover and freeze until firm.

Combine sugar and next 4 ingredients in a saucepan. Bring to a boil over medium heat. Add peach slices; cook 5 minutes or until thoroughly heated.

Spoon ½ cup peach mixture into each of six dessert bowls. Top each serving with ¼ cup cinnamon ice cream and 1 teaspoon pecans. Serve immediately. Yield: 6 servings.

PER SERVING: 157 CALORIES (28% FROM FAT)
FAT 4.8G (SATURATED FAT 1.4G)
PROTEIN 2.3G CARBOHYDRATE 28.6G
CHOLESTEROL 5MG SODIUM 71MG

Spiced Peaches with Cinnamon Ice Cream

FAST, FRESH FAMILY SUPPER

(pictured on page 10)

The flavors in this menu will remind you of a time when supper revolved around vegetables fresh from the garden. The only difference is that these easy recipes are designed for the way we cook today—in a hurry. To save time, sauté the pork and peppers while you cook the potatoes and steam the broccoli. You can heat up the chocolate sauce at the last minute to serve over nonfat ice cream.

Pork and Pepper Skillet

Garlic Mashed Potatoes

Broccoli with Lemon

Chocolate-Mint Sundaes

Serves 4
TOTAL CALORIES PER SERVING: 559
(CALORIES FROM FAT: 26%)

PORK AND PEPPER SKILLET

8 (2-ounce) boneless center-cut pork loin chops
½ teaspoon chopped fresh thyme
¼ teaspoon freshly ground pepper
⅛ teaspoon salt
Vegetable cooking spray
1 teaspoon olive oil
½ medium onion, sliced lengthwise
3 medium-size sweet red peppers, seeded and
    sliced into thin strips
1 clove garlic, crushed
1 tablespoon red wine vinegar
Fresh thyme sprigs (optional)

Rub both sides of pork with chopped thyme, ground pepper, and salt. Coat a large nonstick skillet with cooking spray. Place over medium-high heat until hot. Add pork, and cook 2 to 3 minutes on each side or until lightly browned. Remove pork from skillet; set aside, and keep warm.

Add oil to skillet. Place over medium-high heat until hot. Add onion and sweet red pepper; sauté 5 minutes or until crisp-tender. Add garlic and pork; cover, reduce heat, and cook 10 minutes or until vegetables are tender and pork is done. Drizzle with vinegar. Garnish with thyme sprigs, if desired. Yield: 4 servings.

PER SERVING: 230 CALORIES (39% FROM FAT)
FAT 9.9G (SATURATED FAT 2.4G)
PROTEIN 26.2G   CARBOHYDRATE 8.3G
CHOLESTEROL 71MG   SODIUM 149MG

GARLIC MASHED POTATOES

4½ cups peeled, cubed baking potato
4 cloves garlic
1 bay leaf
¾ cup plain low-fat yogurt
½ cup skim milk
¼ teaspoon salt

Place first 3 ingredients in a saucepan; add water to cover. Bring to a boil; cover, reduce heat, and simmer 15 minutes or until potato is tender.

Drain potato cubes; remove garlic and bay leaf. Mash garlic into a paste; discard bay leaf. Mash potato cubes. Add garlic, yogurt, milk, and salt to mashed potatoes; stir well. Serve immediately. Yield: 4 (1-cup) servings.

PER SERVING: 143 CALORIES (6% FROM FAT)
FAT 0.9G (SATURATED FAT 0.5G)
PROTEIN 7.9G CARBOHYDRATE 27.0G
CHOLESTEROL 3MG SODIUM 210MG

BROCCOLI WITH LEMON

1 pound fresh broccoli
3 tablespoons canned low-sodium chicken broth, undiluted
1 tablespoon lemon juice
1½ teaspoons olive oil
¼ teaspoon salt
⅛ teaspoon freshly ground pepper
Lemon wedges (optional)

Remove broccoli leaves, and cut off tough ends of stalks; discard. Wash broccoli; cut into spears. Arrange broccoli in a steamer basket over boiling water. Cover and steam 5 to 8 minutes. Drain.

Combine broth and next 4 ingredients. Add broccoli; toss. Serve with lemon wedges, if desired. Yield: 4 (1-cup) servings.

PER SERVING: 44 CALORIES (43% FROM FAT)
FAT 2.1G (SATURATED FAT 0.3G)
PROTEIN 3.0G CARBOHYDRATE 5.3G
CHOLESTEROL 0MG SODIUM 175MG

CHOCOLATE-MINT SUNDAES

You may substitute 1 tablespoon water and ¼ teaspoon peppermint extract for the crème de menthe.

2 tablespoons sugar
1½ tablespoons unsweetened cocoa
1 teaspoon cornstarch
¼ cup plus 2 tablespoons water
1 tablespoon crème de menthe
½ teaspoon vanilla extract
2 cups vanilla nonfat ice cream

Combine first 3 ingredients in a small saucepan. Stir in water. Bring to a boil over medium heat, stirring constantly. Stir in crème de menthe and vanilla.

Cook, stirring constantly, 1 minute. Scoop ½ cup ice cream into each of four dessert dishes. Spoon sauce evenly over ice cream. Yield: 4 servings.

PER SERVING: 142 CALORIES (20% FROM FAT)
FAT 3.1G (SATURATED FAT 1.9G)
PROTEIN 3.1G CARBOHYDRATE 24.4G
CHOLESTEROL 9MG SODIUM 57MG

Chocolate-Mint Sundae

Crispy Herbed Chicken

SIMPLE CHICKEN SUPPER

In the days before fat grams were an issue, fried chicken was a standard menu item for many families. You can recapture the taste of old-fashioned fried chicken in this updated recipe that's not only healthier but easier, too. There's no deep-fat fryer and hot grease to worry about! Serve the chicken with an appetizing turnip dish, and prepare easy baked apples as a second side dish or dessert.

Crispy Herbed Chicken
Savory Creamed Turnips
Sugar- and Spice-Baked Apples

Serves 6
TOTAL CALORIES PER SERVING: 441
(CALORIES FROM FAT: 13%)

CRISPY HERBED CHICKEN

This winning replacement for fried chicken is healthier and eliminates messy frying. The secret to a crispy outer coating is to bake the chicken at 400° instead of the usual 350° on a rack in a roasting pan.

1¼ cups soft whole wheat breadcrumbs
1½ tablespoons minced fresh parsley
1½ teaspoons grated lemon rind
1 tablespoon chopped fresh basil
½ teaspoon salt
½ teaspoon pepper
3 tablespoons nonfat buttermilk
¾ teaspoon lemon juice
6 (6-ounce) skinned chicken breast halves
Vegetable cooking spray
Lemon slices (optional)
Fresh parsley sprigs (optional)

Combine first 6 ingredients in a large heavy-duty, zip-top plastic bag; seal bag, and shake well.

Combine buttermilk and lemon juice; brush both sides of chicken with buttermilk mixture. Place chicken in bag; seal bag, and shake until chicken is well coated.

Place chicken on a rack in a roasting pan coated with cooking spray. Sprinkle any remaining breadcrumb mixture over chicken.

Bake chicken, uncovered, at 400° for 40 to 45 minutes or until chicken is tender. If desired, garnish chicken with lemon slices and parsley sprigs. Yield: 6 servings.

PER SERVING: 167 CALORIES (11% FROM FAT)
FAT 2.0G (SATURATED FAT 0.5G)
PROTEIN 29.5G   CARBOHYDRATE 6.5G
CHOLESTEROL 71MG   SODIUM 345MG

SAVORY CREAMED TURNIPS

1½ pounds turnips, diced
½ cup chopped onion
2 cloves garlic, minced
1 tablespoon reduced-calorie stick margarine
1 tablespoon plus 1 teaspoon all-purpose flour
1 cup skim milk
1 teaspoon minced fresh thyme
¼ teaspoon ground white pepper
⅛ teaspoon salt

Combine first 3 ingredients in a medium sauce-pan; add water to cover. Bring to a boil; cover, reduce heat, and simmer 10 to 12 minutes or until turnips are tender. Drain well, and set aside.

Melt margarine in a large heavy saucepan over medium heat. Add flour; cook, stirring constantly, 1 minute. Gradually add milk; cook, stirring constantly, until mixture is thickened and bubbly.

Remove from heat; stir in thyme, pepper, and salt. Add turnip mixture, tossing gently to combine. Serve immediately. Yield: 6 servings.

PER SERVING: 68 CALORIES (19% FROM FAT)
FAT 1.4G (SATURATED FAT 0.3G)
PROTEIN 2.7G CARBOHYDRATE 11.8G
CHOLESTEROL 1MG SODIUM 163MG

Fat Alert

If you're trying to cut back on fat, don't forget to switch the milk you use. Whole milk may be labeled as containing only 3.5 to 3.7 percent fat by weight, but an 8-ounce serving actually has 8 grams of fat. Think 2 percent milk is the lean alternative? Wrong. This milk still contains about 5 grams of fat per 8-ounce serving. For a low-fat diet, choose at least 1 percent low-fat milk or preferably skim milk.

SUGAR- AND SPICE-BAKED APPLES

6 medium cooking apples
¼ cup plus 2 tablespoons raisins
¼ cup firmly packed brown sugar
½ teaspoon ground cinnamon
½ teaspoon ground nutmeg
2 tablespoons reduced-calorie margarine
1 cup unsweetened apple juice

Core apples to within ½ inch from bottom; peel top third of each apple. Combine raisins and next 3 ingredients in a small bowl; spoon mixture evenly into cavities of apples. Place apples in a 10- x 6- x 2-inch baking dish. Top each apple with 1 tea-spoon margarine; pour apple juice over apples.

Cover and bake at 350° for 35 to 40 minutes or until apples are tender, basting occasionally with juice. Yield: 6 servings.

PER SERVING: 206 CALORIES (14% FROM FAT)
FAT 3.2G (SATURATED FAT 0.5G)
PROTEIN 0.6G CARBOHYDRATE 47.8G
CHOLESTEROL 0MG SODIUM 42MG

Microwave Directions: Core apples to within ½ inch from bottom; peel top third of each apple. Combine raisins and next 3 ingredients; spoon mix-ture evenly into cavities of apples. Place apples in a 10- x 6- x 2-inch microwave-safe dish. Top each apple with 1 teaspoon margarine; pour apple juice evenly over apples.

Cover with heavy-duty plastic wrap, and fold back a corner to vent. Microwave at HIGH 10 to 12 minutes or until apples are tender, basting with juice and rotating dish a quarter-turn every 2 min-utes. Let stand, covered, 5 minutes before serving.

SEAFOOD IN A SNAP

Easy to prepare, loaded with flavor, yet low in fat and calories—
what more could you want? Fish is always a good entrée when time
is a consideration. Here it's served with a simple rice dish and stir-
fried vegetables. Dessert is up to you. You may want to serve fresh
fruit or ½ cup nonfat frozen yogurt, adding another 90 calories or so.

Gingered Flounder

Almond-Rice Pilaf

Sesame Broccoli and Carrots

Serves 4
TOTAL CALORIES PER SERVING: 486
(CALORIES FROM FAT: 16%)

Gingered Flounder, Almond-Rice Pilaf, and Sesame Broccoli and Carrots

GINGERED FLOUNDER

¾ cup peeled, coarsely grated gingerroot
2 tablespoons low-sodium soy sauce
2 tablespoons dry sherry
2 tablespoons lemon juice
2 teaspoons sugar
4 (4-ounce) flounder fillets
Vegetable cooking spray
1 teaspoon dark sesame oil

Place gingerroot on several layers of damp cheese-cloth. Gather edges of cheesecloth together; squeeze bag over a bowl to extract 3 tablespoons gingerroot juice. Combine 2 tablespoons gingerroot juice, soy sauce, and next 3 ingredients in a dish; add fish, turning to coat. Cover and chill 20 minutes; turn once. Remove from marinade, discarding marinade.

Place fish on rack of a broiler pan coated with cooking spray; broil 5½ inches from heat (with electric oven door partially opened) 3 minutes or until lightly browned (do not turn). Brush oil over fish; broil 1 minute or until fish flakes easily when tested with a fork. Place fish on individual serving plates; drizzle remaining 1 tablespoon gingerroot juice over fish. Yield: 4 (3-ounce) servings.

PER SERVING: 191 CALORIES (19% FROM FAT)
FAT 4.0G (SATURATED FAT 0.7G)
PROTEIN 31.0G CARBOHYDRATE 5.0G
CHOLESTEROL 87MG SODIUM 427MG

ALMOND-RICE PILAF

4 cups hot cooked rice (cooked without salt or fat)
¼ cup sliced green onions
2 tablespoons sliced almonds, toasted
1 teaspoon low-sodium soy sauce
¼ teaspoon salt

Combine all ingredients; toss well. Serve hot. Yield: 4 (1-cup) servings.

PER SERVING: 222 CALORIES (9% FROM FAT)
FAT 2.3G (SATURATED FAT 0.3G)
PROTEIN 4.8G CARBOHYDRATE 44.1G
CHOLESTEROL 0MG SODIUM 185MG

SESAME BROCCOLI AND CARROTS

5 cups broccoli flowerets
1 cup julienne-sliced carrot
¼ cup canned low-sodium chicken broth, undiluted
1 teaspoon cornstarch
1½ tablespoons low-sodium soy sauce
1½ tablespoons dry sherry
1 teaspoon vegetable oil
1 tablespoon peeled, minced gingerroot
2 cloves garlic, minced
½ teaspoon dark sesame oil
1 teaspoon sesame seeds, toasted

Cook broccoli and carrot, covered, in boiling water in a large Dutch oven 3 minutes. Drain and rinse with cold water. Drain well.

Combine broth and next 3 ingredients in a small bowl; stir well, and set aside.

Drizzle vegetable oil in a wok or large nonstick skillet, coating sides. Heat at medium-high (375°) until hot. Add gingerroot and garlic; stir-fry 10 seconds. Add broccoli and carrot; stir-fry 1 minute. Add broth mixture; bring to a boil, and cook, stirring constantly, 1 minute or until thickened. Remove from heat; stir in sesame oil, and sprinkle with sesame seeds. Yield: 4 (1-cup) servings.

PER SERVING: 73 CALORIES (32% FROM FAT)
FAT 2.6G (SATURATED FAT 0.4G)
PROTEIN 4.0G CARBOHYDRATE 10.4G
CHOLESTEROL 0MG SODIUM 191MG

Cook's Tip

Successful cooks know that meal preparation goes more smoothly when they take time up front to get organized. Always look over your recipes and assemble your ingredients first. For instance, you'll need gingerroot in two of the recipes above, so when you get out the gingerroot, peel enough for both.

Hearty Three-Bean Chili and Confetti Corn Muffins

A NIGHT FOR MEMORIES

Why wait for a formal class reunion to visit with old school chums? Invite them to relive those bright years and to enjoy this make-ahead menu soon.

Sassy Snack Mix (½-cup serving per person) and Confetti Corn Muffins (one per person) can be made in advance and stored in air-tight containers. The chili and coleslaw can be refrigerated for a day.

Sassy Snack Mix

Hearty Three-Bean Chili

Creamy Coleslaw

Confetti Corn Muffins

Sparkling water

Serves 8
TOTAL CALORIES PER SERVING: 706
(CALORIES FROM FAT: 16%)

SASSY SNACK MIX

You can substitute raisins or chopped dried apricots or peaches for the dried cherries in this recipe.

2 cups crispy corn cereal squares
2 cups crispy whole wheat cereal squares
2 cups small fat-free pretzels
1½ cups oyster crackers
3 tablespoons margarine, melted
1 tablespoon low-sodium Worcestershire sauce
½ teaspoon Creole seasoning
1 cup dried cherries

Combine first 4 ingredients in a large bowl. Combine margarine, Worcestershire sauce, and Creole seasoning; drizzle over cereal mixture, tossing well.

Spread cereal mixture in a 15- x 10- x 1-inch jellyroll pan. Bake at 325° for 15 to 18 minutes or until golden, stirring once. Cool completely, and transfer to a serving bowl. Add cherries, and toss gently. Yield: 14 (½-cup) servings.

PER SERVING: 178 CALORIES (18% FROM FAT)
FAT 3.6G (SATURATED FAT 0.6G)
PROTEIN 3.4G CARBOHYDRATE 34.6G
CHOLESTEROL 0MG SODIUM 410MG

HEARTY THREE-BEAN CHILI

1 teaspoon vegetable oil
2 cups chopped onion
3 cloves garlic, minced
2 tablespoons chili powder
1½ tablespoons ground cumin
½ teaspoon salt
½ cup water
2 (14½-ounce) cans no-salt-added stewed tomatoes, undrained
2 (15-ounce) cans black beans, drained
1 (16-ounce) can kidney beans, drained
1 (15-ounce) can pinto beans, drained
1 (14¼-ounce) can no-salt-added beef broth
1 large green pepper, seeded and cut into 1-inch pieces
1 large sweet red pepper, seeded and cut into 1-inch pieces
½ cup nonfat sour cream
⅓ cup diced green pepper
⅓ cup diced sweet red pepper

Heat oil in a Dutch oven over medium-high heat until hot. Add onion and garlic; sauté 5 minutes or until onion is tender. Stir in chili powder, cumin, and salt; sauté 1 minute. Add water and next 7 ingredients. Bring mixture to a boil; cover, reduce heat, and simmer 30 minutes, stirring occasionally.

Ladle chili into eight individual bowls; top each serving with 1 tablespoon sour cream. Sprinkle diced green and red pepper evenly over servings. Yield: 8 (1½-cup) servings.

PER SERVING: 276 CALORIES (13% FROM FAT)
FAT 3.9G (SATURATED FAT 1.5G)
PROTEIN 14.7G CARBOHYDRATE 48.3G
CHOLESTEROL 6MG SODIUM 535MG

CREAMY COLESLAW

Save time by using a food processor to chop the cabbage and shred the carrot.

6¾ cups chopped cabbage (about 1 medium)
1½ cups shredded carrot
1 cup reduced-fat mayonnaise
1 cup nonfat sour cream
¼ cup sugar
¼ cup prepared horseradish
1½ tablespoons fresh lemon juice
½ teaspoon dry mustard
¼ teaspoon salt
¼ teaspoon celery seeds
¼ teaspoon garlic powder
⅛ teaspoon ground white pepper
⅛ teaspoon ground red pepper

Combine cabbage and carrot in a large bowl.
Position knife blade in food processor bowl; add mayonnaise and remaining 10 ingredients. Process 15 seconds or until smooth. Pour mayonnaise mixture over cabbage mixture; toss gently. Cover and chill at least 8 hours. Toss gently before serving. Yield: 8 (¾-cup) servings.

PER SERVING: 133 CALORIES (16% FROM FAT)
FAT 2.3G (SATURATED FAT 0.0G)
PROTEIN 3.6G   CARBOHYDRATE 25.0G
CHOLESTEROL 0MG   SODIUM 407MG

CONFETTI CORN MUFFINS

1¼ cups all-purpose flour
2 teaspoons baking powder
¼ teaspoon salt
¾ cup yellow cornmeal
1 tablespoon sugar
¼ teaspoon ground red pepper
1 egg, lightly beaten
1 cup nonfat buttermilk
2 tablespoons margarine, melted
½ cup diced sweet red pepper
⅓ cup thinly sliced green onions
1 tablespoon seeded, minced jalapeño pepper
Vegetable cooking spray

Combine first 6 ingredients in a medium bowl; make a well in center of mixture. Combine egg, buttermilk, and margarine; add to flour mixture, stirring just until dry ingredients are moistened. Fold in diced red pepper, green onions, and jalapeño pepper.
Spoon batter into muffin pans coated with cooking spray, filling two-thirds full. Bake at 400° for 28 to 30 minutes or until golden. Remove from pans immediately. Yield: 12 muffins.

PER MUFFIN: 119 CALORIES (22% FROM FAT)
FAT 2.9G (SATURATED FAT 0.6G)
PROTEIN 3.5G   CARBOHYDRATE 19.6G
CHOLESTEROL 19MG   SODIUM 99MG

Which Cornmeal for You?

Most cornmeal is made from either yellow or white corn, which determines its color. Preference for a particular color cornmeal is regional. Most Southerners prefer milder-tasting white cornmeal, while yellow is generally favored in the North. You can use them interchangeably in recipes.

Self-rising cornmeal is the same as regular white or yellow cornmeal, but it contains leavening agents and salt.

Whole grain cornmeal is often ground the old-fashioned way, between massive millstones at a gristmill. Cornmeal ground this way (called stone-ground) has a coarser texture than commercially ground cornmeal. (Store whole grain cornmeal in the refrigerator or freezer to prevent spoilage.)

In the American Southwest, traditional breads may be prepared with blue cornmeal, which is bluish gray and fairly coarse in texture.

32

Bacon, Lettuce, and Tomato Salad (recipe on page 43)

DAYTIME FARE

*Y*oung Sally's idea of breakfast is a bowl of brightly colored O's floating in milk, and Jimmy defines the word lunch as a creamy peanut butter and jelly sandwich. But breakfast and lunch entrées can be more varied than that, even with the under-ten crowd. In the pages that follow, you'll find recipes for healthy French toast, biscuits, pancakes, and several egg dishes. Lunch suggestions include main-dish salads, sandwiches, and pizzas.

Daytime is a good time to involve children in meal preparation. For instance, they can help measure and stir the ingredients for Swiss Muesli (page 34) and assemble the Ham and Apple Sandwiches (page 48). Who knows? They may even learn to enjoy food other than cereal and peanut butter.

Swiss Muesli

1½ cups regular oats, uncooked
1½ cups skim milk
2 tablespoons brown sugar
2 tablespoons raisins
⅛ teaspoon salt
1 cup vanilla low-fat yogurt
2 tablespoons chopped pecans

Combine first 5 ingredients in a medium bowl, stirring well. Cover and chill 8 hours. Stir in yogurt. Spoon into individual bowls; sprinkle evenly with chopped pecans. Yield: 4 (¾-cup) servings.

PER SERVING: 262 CALORIES (22% FROM FAT)
FAT 6.4G (SATURATED FAT 1.2G)
PROTEIN 11.3G CARBOHYDRATE 41.4G
CHOLESTEROL 5MG SODIUM 159MG

Quick French Toast

4 (1-ounce) Vienna or French bread slices
Vegetable cooking spray
1 cup skim milk
¾ cup fat-free egg substitute
1 tablespoon sugar
½ teaspoon vanilla extract
Dash of salt
2 teaspoons cinnamon sugar
3 tablespoons maple syrup

Cut each bread slice diagonally into 4 triangles, and arrange triangles in a medium-size nonstick skillet coated with cooking spray. Combine milk and next 4 ingredients; pour over bread.

Cover and cook over medium heat 11 minutes or until set. Remove from heat; sprinkle with cinnamon sugar. Cut into 3 wedges, and drizzle 1 tablespoon syrup over each wedge. Yield: 3 servings.

Note: Make your own cinnamon sugar by combining one part ground cinnamon to two parts sugar.

PER SERVING: 248 CALORIES (4% FROM FAT)
FAT 1.2G (SATURATED FAT 0.4G)
PROTEIN 12.2G CARBOHYDRATE 45.5G
CHOLESTEROL 3MG SODIUM 403MG

Drop Biscuits with Sausage Gravy

1 cup all-purpose flour
1½ teaspoons baking powder
⅛ teaspoon salt
½ cup skim milk
1 teaspoon margarine, melted
Vegetable cooking spray
Sausage Gravy

Combine first 3 ingredients in a bowl. Combine milk and margarine; add to dry ingredients, stirring just until dry ingredients are moistened.

Drop batter by heaping tablespoons onto a baking sheet coated with cooking spray to make 6 biscuits. Bake at 450° for 11 minutes or until golden. Split biscuits; top evenly with Sausage Gravy. Yield: 6 servings.

Sausage Gravy
1 tablespoon margarine
½ pound bulk turkey breakfast sausage
3 tablespoons all-purpose flour
2¼ cups skim milk
½ teaspoon pepper
⅛ teaspoon salt

Melt margarine in a medium saucepan over medium heat; add sausage. Cook until sausage is browned, stirring until it crumbles. Sprinkle sausage with flour; cook, stirring constantly, 1 minute. Gradually add milk, stirring until well blended. Cook, stirring constantly, over medium heat 8 minutes or until thickened. Remove from heat; stir in pepper and salt. Yield: 3 cups.

Note: Look for the sausage in the fresh meat or freezer section of the grocery store.

PER SERVING: 201 CALORIES (18% FROM FAT)
FAT 4.1G (SATURATED FAT 1.0G)
PROTEIN 12.4G CARBOHYDRATE 28.1G
CHOLESTEROL 19MG SODIUM 506MG

RISE AND SHINE ENGLISH MUFFINS

2 teaspoons reduced-calorie margarine, divided
4 (1-ounce) slices turkey ham
1 cup fat-free egg substitute
4 (¾-ounce) slices reduced-fat American cheese
4 whole wheat English muffins, split and toasted

Melt 1 teaspoon margarine in a large nonstick skillet over medium heat. Add turkey ham; cook 1 minute on each side or until lightly browned. Remove from skillet; set aside, and keep warm.

Melt remaining 1 teaspoon margarine in skillet over medium heat. Add egg substitute; cook 45 seconds or until set, stirring occasionally. Place 1 cheese slice on each of 4 muffin halves. Place egg substitute mixture evenly over cheese; top with turkey ham and remaining muffin halves. Yield: 4 servings.

PER SERVING: 300 CALORIES (21% FROM FAT)
FAT 7.0G (SATURATED FAT 2.9G)
PROTEIN 21.5G   CARBOHYDRATE 38.2G
CHOLESTEROL 10MG   SODIUM 864MG

OATMEAL-BUTTERMILK PANCAKES

1¼ cups low-fat buttermilk
½ cup quick-cooking oats
½ teaspoon vanilla extract
1 tablespoon vegetable oil
1 egg, lightly beaten
1¼ cups all-purpose flour
2 tablespoons brown sugar
½ teaspoon baking soda
½ teaspoon salt
Maple syrup (optional)

Combine first 3 ingredients; let stand 10 minutes, stirring occasionally. Stir in oil and egg.

Combine flour and next 3 ingredients in a large bowl; stir well. Add oat mixture to flour mixture, stirring until smooth.

For each pancake, spoon about ⅓ cup batter onto a hot nonstick griddle or skillet. Cook pancakes until tops are covered with bubbles and edges look cooked. Turn pancakes, and cook other sides. Serve pancakes with syrup, if desired. Yield: 8 pancakes.

PER PANCAKE: 144 CALORIES (22% FROM FAT)
FAT 3.5G (SATURATED FAT 1.1G)
PROTEIN 5.1G   CARBOHYDRATE 23.0G
CHOLESTEROL 28MG   SODIUM 255MG

Perfect Pancakes

Packaged mixes for pancakes are easy to prepare, but with just a few extra minutes, you can make delicious pancakes from scratch. The flavor and texture of homemade pancakes are well worth the effort, especially when you have overnight guests for breakfast.

Use a nonstick griddle to keep the pancakes as fat free as possible. If using a regular griddle, coat the surface with vegetable cooking spray before heating.

If you have any leftovers, place wax paper between cooled pancakes. Then wrap the pancakes tightly in aluminum foil, and freeze them up to one month.

How do you know when it's flipping time? As soon as the top surface of a pancake is full of bubbles and the edges begin to look cooked, it's ready to turn. The second side will take only a minute or two to brown.

Whole Wheat-Apple Pancakes with Apple Topping

WHOLE WHEAT-APPLE PANCAKES WITH APPLE TOPPING

½ cup all-purpose flour
½ cup whole wheat flour
1 teaspoon baking soda
⅛ teaspoon salt
1 tablespoon sugar
1 egg, lightly beaten
1 cup nonfat buttermilk
2 teaspoons vegetable oil
½ cup peeled, finely chopped apple
Vegetable cooking spray
Apple Topping

Combine first 5 ingredients in a medium bowl; make a well in center of mixture.

Combine egg, buttermilk, and oil; add to flour mixture, stirring just until dry ingredients are moistened. Stir in apple.

For each pancake, pour ¼ cup batter onto a hot griddle or skillet coated with cooking spray, spreading batter to a 4-inch circle. Cook pancakes until tops are covered with bubbles and edges look cooked; turn pancakes, and cook other sides. To serve, top each pancake with 1½ tablespoons Apple Topping. Yield: 10 pancakes.

APPLE TOPPING
½ cup unsweetened applesauce
½ cup reduced-calorie apple jelly
½ teaspoon apple pie spice

Combine all ingredients in a small saucepan. Cook over low heat until jelly melts, stirring occasionally. Yield: 1 cup.

PER PANCAKE: 109 CALORIES (15% FROM FAT)
FAT 1.8G (SATURATED FAT 0.4G)
PROTEIN 3.2G   CARBOHYDRATE 20.7G
CHOLESTEROL 23MG   SODIUM 203MG

BLUEBERRY WAFFLES

1¾ cups all-purpose flour
1 tablespoon baking powder
Dash of salt
2 egg whites, lightly beaten
1 egg, lightly beaten
1¾ cups skim milk
3 tablespoons vegetable oil
Vegetable cooking spray
1 cup fresh or frozen blueberries, divided
Maple Syrup (optional)
Additional blueberries (optional)

Combine first 3 ingredients in a medium bowl; stir well. Combine egg whites and next 3 ingredients in a small bowl; stir well. Add to flour mixture, stirring until well blended.

Coat a waffle iron with cooking spray; allow waffle iron to preheat. Spoon about ⅓ cup batter per waffle onto hot waffle iron, spreading batter to edges. Spoon 2 tablespoons blueberries per waffle evenly over batter. Bake 6 to 7 minutes or until steaming stops. Serve with syrup, if desired. Garnish with additional blueberries, if desired. Yield: 8 (4-inch) waffles.

Note: If you use frozen blueberries, do not thaw them before adding to batter.

PER WAFFLE: 189 CALORIES (30% FROM FAT)
FAT 6.3G (SATURATED FAT 1.2G)
PROTEIN 6.4G   CARBOHYDRATE 26.7G
CHOLESTEROL 29MG   SODIUM 86MG

FYI

The amount of batter you pour onto your waffle iron depends on how large the iron is. It's best to check the manufacturer's directions for specific amounts of batter to use for each waffle.

BREAKFAST BURRITOS

6 (6-inch) flour tortillas
2 cups fat-free egg substitute
¾ cup plus 2 tablespoons taco sauce, divided
¼ cup water
2 tablespoons canned chopped green chiles, drained
¼ teaspoon salt
Dash of pepper
Vegetable cooking spray
½ cup plus 1 tablespoon shredded reduced-fat sharp Cheddar cheese, divided

Wrap tortillas in aluminum foil. Bake at 350° for 7 minutes. Set tortillas aside, and keep warm.

Combine egg substitute, 2 tablespoons taco sauce, and next 4 ingredients in a medium bowl; stir well. Coat a large nonstick skillet with cooking spray; place over medium heat until hot. Add egg substitute mixture; cook until mixture is softly set, stirring often.

Spoon mixture evenly over tortillas. Top each with 1 tablespoon of remaining taco sauce and 1 tablespoon cheese; roll up tortillas. Arrange burritos on a serving platter, and top evenly with remaining taco sauce and cheese. Yield: 6 servings.

PER SERVING: 232 CALORIES (17% FROM FAT)
FAT 4.3G (SATURATED FAT 1.7G)
PROTEIN 13.5G CARBOHYDRATE 34.9G
CHOLESTEROL 7MG SODIUM 498MG

HERBED POTATO FRITTATA

2 cups diced red potato
1 tablespoon reduced-calorie stick margarine
⅓ cup sliced green onions
1 teaspoon dried basil
½ teaspoon dried marjoram
¼ teaspoon salt
¼ teaspoon pepper
1 clove garlic, minced
2 (8-ounce) cartons fat-free egg substitute
¾ cup (3 ounces) shredded reduced-fat sharp Cheddar cheese

Place potato in a saucepan. Add water to cover; bring to a boil. Cover, reduce heat, and simmer 15 minutes or until tender; drain. Melt margarine in a 10-inch nonstick skillet over medium-high heat. Add potato, onions, and next 5 ingredients; sauté 2 minutes. Spread evenly in skillet; pour egg substitute over potato mixture. Reduce heat to medium-low; cook, uncovered, 8 minutes or until almost set.

Wrap handle of skillet with aluminum foil; broil 5½ inches from heat (with electric oven door partially opened) 3 minutes. Sprinkle with cheese; broil 30 additional seconds or until cheese melts. Yield: 4 servings.

PER SERVING: 274 CALORIES (24% FROM FAT)
FAT 7.4G (SATURATED FAT 3.5G)
PROTEIN 25.6G CARBOHYDRATE 26.1G
CHOLESTEROL 19MG SODIUM 681MG

Did You Know?

A frittata is Italy's version of the French omelet. While a cooked omelet is folded over vegetables, meat, or cheese, a frittata is made by pouring the eggs over those extra ingredients before cooking. A frittata also tends to be firmer than an omelet and is round, not folded.

QUICK AND EASY QUICHE

1 cup fat-free egg substitute
1 cup water
½ cup low-fat buttermilk biscuit and baking
   mix
½ cup instant nonfat dry milk powder
½ cup plain nonfat yogurt
2 tablespoons freshly grated Parmesan cheese
½ teaspoon dry mustard
¼ teaspoon hot sauce
1 cup (4 ounces) shredded reduced-fat sharp
   Cheddar cheese
¾ cup diced low-salt, reduced-fat ham
½ cup chopped green onions
Vegetable cooking spray
Green onions (optional)
Fresh strawberries (optional)

Position knife blade in food processor bowl; add first 8 ingredients. Process 1 minute or until smooth.

Combine egg substitute mixture, Cheddar cheese, ham, and chopped green onions in a medium bowl; stir well. Pour mixture into 9-inch pieplate coated with cooking spray.

Bake at 350° for 40 minutes or until set. Let stand 5 minutes before serving. Cut into wedges. If desired, garnish with green onions and strawberries. Yield: 6 servings.

PER SERVING: 159 CALORIES (30% FROM FAT)
FAT 5.3G (SATURATED FAT 2.9G)
PROTEIN 18.3G CARBOHYDRATE 9.2G
CHOLESTEROL 25MG SODIUM 437MG

Quick and Easy Quiche

Vegetable Omelets

VEGETABLE OMELETS

3 small round red potatoes
Vegetable cooking spray
1½ teaspoons vegetable oil
1 cup sliced fresh mushrooms
¾ cup chopped fresh broccoli
½ cup chopped onion
½ cup chopped sweet red pepper
1 tablespoon chopped fresh basil
¼ teaspoon freshly ground pepper
1 cup fat-free egg substitute
2 tablespoons unsweetened orange juice
2 egg whites
1 tablespoon all-purpose flour
¾ cup (3 ounces) shredded reduced-fat sharp
    Cheddar cheese, divided
Fresh basil sprigs (optional)

Cook potatoes in boiling water to cover 15 minutes or just until tender. Drain; cool. Cut potatoes into thin slices.

Coat a medium-size nonstick skillet with cooking spray; add oil. Place over medium-high heat until hot. Add mushrooms and next 3 ingredients; sauté 6 minutes or until vegetables are tender. Add potato slices, chopped basil, and ¼ teaspoon pepper; cook 1 minute. Set aside, and keep warm.

Combine egg substitute and orange juice; beat at medium speed of an electric mixer until foamy. Beat egg whites at high speed of mixer until soft peaks form. Add flour to beaten egg whites; beat until stiff peaks form. Gently fold egg white mixture into egg substitute mixture.

Coat a medium-size nonstick skillet with cooking spray; place over medium heat until hot. Add one-third of egg mixture to skillet; spread evenly. Cover and cook 4 minutes or until set.

Spoon one-third of vegetable mixture over half of omelet. Sprinkle with ¼ cup shredded cheese. Loosen omelet with a spatula; fold in half. Slide onto a serving platter; set aside. Repeat procedure twice. To serve, cut each omelet in half. Garnish with fresh basil sprigs, if desired. Yield: 6 servings.

PER SERVING: 125 CALORIES (30% FROM FAT)
FAT 4.2G (SATURATED FAT 1.8G)
PROTEIN 10.9G CARBOHYDRATE 11.2G
CHOLESTEROL 9MG SODIUM 186MG

SAUSAGE AND EGG CASSEROLE

1 pound bulk turkey breakfast sausage
3 cups cubed white bread
2 cups skim milk
1½ cups fat-free egg substitute
½ cup (2 ounces) shredded reduced-fat sharp
    Cheddar cheese
1 teaspoon dry mustard
Vegetable cooking spray

Cook sausage in a large nonstick skillet over medium-high heat until browned, stirring until it crumbles. Drain well.

Combine sausage, bread cubes, and next 4 ingredients; stir well. Pour into in a 13- x 9- x 2-inch baking dish coated with cooking spray. Bake, uncovered, at 350° for 45 minutes or until a wooden pick inserted in center of mixture comes out clean. Yield: 9 servings.

PER SERVING: 157 CALORIES (27% FROM FAT)
FAT 4.7G (SATURATED FAT 1.7G)
PROTEIN 14.4G CARBOHYDRATE 13.1G
CHOLESTEROL 23MG SODIUM 471MG

Menu Helper

For an easy low-fat sauce to serve over fresh berries, combine 1 cup sliced fresh or frozen peaches, ¼ cup low-fat sour cream, 1 tablespoon brown sugar, and ½ teaspoon lemon juice in the container of an electric blender; cover and process until the mixture is smooth.

Fruit and Cheese Platter

FRUIT AND CHEESE PLATTER

½ cup commercial fat-free honey-mustard
    dressing
⅓ cup plain nonfat yogurt
2 tablespoons raspberry vinegar
2 teaspoons sugar
3 cups fresh strawberries, halved
2¼ cups fresh blueberries
1½ cups seedless green grapes
1½ cups julienne-sliced jicama
1¼ cups (6 ounces) cubed nonfat Cheddar
    cheese
24 (¼-inch-thick) slices cantaloupe (about 1½
    medium)
Fresh strawberry halves (optional)
Fresh mint sprigs (optional)

Combine first 4 ingredients. Cover and chill.
  Place chilled dressing in a small bowl on a large
serving platter. Arrange 3 cups strawberry halves
and next 5 ingredients on platter. If desired, garnish with strawberry halves and fresh mint sprigs.
Yield: 6 servings.

PER SERVING: 237 CALORIES (5% FROM FAT)
FAT 1.3G (SATURATED FAT 0.4G)
PROTEIN 13.2G CARBOHYDRATE 47.3G
CHOLESTEROL 5MG SODIUM 411MG

Here are some ideas for healthy salad
sidekicks.
   • breadsticks
   • reduced-fat wheat crackers
   • low-fat croutons
   • French bread
   • Melba toast
   • rice cakes
   • hard rolls
   • baked tortilla chips

BACON, LETTUCE, AND TOMATO SALAD

(pictured on page 32)

8 cups tightly packed torn red leaf lettuce
4 small tomatoes, cut into wedges
6 ounces Canadian bacon, coarsely chopped
4 (1-ounce) slices French bread, cubed and
    toasted
¾ cup (3 ounces) shredded reduced-fat sharp
    Cheddar cheese
4 slices turkey bacon, cooked and coarsely
    crumbled
Tangy French Dressing

Combine first 3 ingredients; toss well. Place mixture evenly on eight individual salad plates.
  Top salads evenly with bread cubes, cheese, and
bacon. Serve each salad with 2 tablespoons Tangy
French Dressing. Yield: 8 (1¼-cup) servings.

TANGY FRENCH DRESSING
½ teaspoon unflavored gelatin
1 tablespoon cold water
¼ cup boiling water
½ cup spicy hot vegetable juice
1½ tablespoons sugar
2 tablespoons cider vinegar
1 tablespoon low-sodium Worcestershire sauce
¼ teaspoon salt
¼ teaspoon dry mustard
⅛ teaspoon garlic powder
Dash of freshly ground pepper

Sprinkle gelatin over cold water; let stand 1
minute. Add boiling water; stir until gelatin dissolves. Set aside.
  Combine vegetable juice and remaining 7 ingredients in container of an electric blender; cover and
process 30 seconds. Add gelatin mixture; process
until well blended. Transfer mixture to a small
bowl; cover and chill thoroughly. Stir well before
serving. Yield: 1 cup.

PER SERVING: 163 CALORIES (30% FROM FAT)
FAT 5.4G (SATURATED FAT 2.1G)
PROTEIN 11.2G CARBOHYDRATE 17.4G
CHOLESTEROL 24MG SODIUM 667MG

Mandarin Turkey Salad

MANDARIN TURKEY SALAD

4½ cups loosely packed torn romaine lettuce
1½ cups loosely packed torn radicchio
1½ cups cubed cooked turkey or chicken
     breast
¼ cup vertically sliced purple onion
1 (11-ounce) can mandarin oranges in light
     syrup, drained
¼ cup unsweetened orange juice
1½ tablespoons red wine vinegar
1½ teaspoons poppy seeds
1½ teaspoons olive oil
¼ teaspoon Dijon mustard
⅛ teaspoon salt
⅛ teaspoon pepper

Combine first 5 ingredients in a large bowl; set salad aside.

Combine orange juice, vinegar, and remaining 5 ingredients in a small jar; cover tightly, and shake vigorously.

Pour orange juice mixture over salad, tossing gently to coat. Serve immediately. Yield: 4 (2-cup) servings.

PER SERVING: 163 CALORIES (23% FROM FAT)
FAT 4.1G (SATURATED FAT 0.8G)
PROTEIN 17.0G   CARBOHYDRATE 14.0G
CHOLESTEROL 36MG   SODIUM 128MG

OPEN-FACE PHILLY CHEESE SANDWICHES

1 teaspoon olive oil
1½ cups sliced onion
1½ cups sliced green pepper
¼ teaspoon ground pepper
4 (1-ounce) slices French bread
Olive oil-flavored cooking spray
8 ounces thinly sliced deli roast beef
4 (1-ounce) slices reduced-fat Swiss cheese

Heat oil in a nonstick skillet over medium heat. Add onion; cook 10 minutes, stirring often. Add green pepper and ground pepper; cook 3 minutes.

Coat 1 side of each bread slice with cooking spray. Top each slice with 2 ounces beef, ¼ cup onion mixture, and 1 slice cheese. Place sandwiches on a baking sheet coated with cooking spray; broil 5½ inches from heat (with electric oven door partially opened) 2 minutes. Yield: 4 servings.

PER SERVING: 291 CALORIES (27% FROM FAT)
FAT 8.6G (SATURATED FAT 3.7G)
PROTEIN 24.8G CARBOHYDRATE 28.4G
CHOLESTEROL 39MG SODIUM 819MG

BARBECUE BEEFWICHES

1 (3-pound) lean beef rump roast
Vegetable cooking spray
1½ cups reduced-calorie ketchup
¼ cup plus 2 tablespoons red wine vinegar
⅓ cup firmly packed dark brown sugar
1 tablespoon dried onion flakes
1 teaspoon liquid smoke
½ teaspoon salt
½ teaspoon pepper
⅛ teaspoon garlic powder
2½ cups finely shredded cabbage
½ cup finely shredded carrot
1½ tablespoons sugar
2 tablespoons white vinegar
2 tablespoons minced sweet pickle
1½ teaspoons vegetable oil
⅛ teaspoon celery seeds
12 hamburger buns, split and toasted

Trim fat from roast. Coat a Dutch oven with cooking spray; place over medium heat until hot. Add roast; cook until browned on all sides, turning often. Remove roast from Dutch oven; wipe drippings from Dutch oven with a paper towel.

Combine ketchup and next 7 ingredients, stirring well. Return roast to Dutch oven, and pour ketchup mixture over roast. Bring to a boil. Cover, reduce heat, and simmer 4 hours or until meat is tender. Remove roast from Dutch oven, reserving sauce in Dutch oven. Let roast cool slightly. Shred meat with two forks, and return to Dutch oven. Cover and cook over medium heat until thoroughly heated, stirring occasionally.

Combine cabbage and carrot. Combine sugar and next 4 ingredients in a saucepan; bring to a boil, stirring occasionally. Boil 1 minute. Pour over cabbage mixture, and toss gently. Spoon about ½ cup meat mixture on bottom half of each bun; top each with ¼ cup cabbage mixture. Cover with bun tops. Yield: 12 servings.

PER SERVING: 325 CALORIES (22% FROM FAT)
FAT 8.0G (SATURATED FAT 1.9G)
PROTEIN 21.1G CARBOHYDRATE 39.9G
CHOLESTEROL 60MG SODIUM 298MG

Barbecue Beefwich

SPICY JOES

(pictured on page 2)

Add either hot or mild chiles to the meat mixture, depending on your preference for heat.

Vegetable cooking spray
½ cup chopped green pepper
¼ cup minced onion
1½ pounds ground round
1¼ cups no-salt-added tomato sauce
¼ cup water
¼ cup reduced-calorie chili sauce
1 tablespoon chili power
½ teaspoon salt
¼ teaspoon freshly ground black pepper
¼ teaspoon ground red pepper
1 (6-ounce) can no-salt-added tomato paste
1 (4-ounce) can chopped green chiles, drained
8 reduced-calorie whole wheat hamburger
    buns

Coat a large nonstick skillet with cooking spray, and place over medium-high heat until hot. Add green pepper and onion; sauté until crisp-tender. Remove pepper mixture from skillet.

Add ground round to skillet, and cook over medium heat until meat is browned, stirring until it crumbles. Drain and pat dry with paper towels. Wipe drippings from skillet with a paper towel.

Return meat mixture and pepper mixture to skillet. Add tomato sauce and next 8 ingredients; stir well. Cook over medium heat 10 minutes or until thoroughly heated, stirring occasionally. Spoon evenly over bottom halves of buns. Cover with bun tops. Serve immediately. Yield: 8 servings.

PER SERVING: 253 CALORIES (23% FROM FAT)
FAT 6.6G (SATURATED FAT 2.2G)
PROTEIN 22.2G CARBOHYDRATE 25.3G
CHOLESTEROL 69MG SODIUM 479MG

BARBECUED CHICKEN SANDWICHES

Use sweet, full-flavored balsamic vinegar for the best flavor in this barbecue sauce.

¾ cup chopped onion
⅔ cup no-salt-added tomato sauce
3 tablespoons sugar
2 tablespoons balsamic vinegar
2 teaspoons garlic powder
1 teaspoon celery seeds
1 teaspoon chili powder
2 teaspoons low-sodium Worcestershire sauce
¼ teaspoon salt
2 cups chopped cooked chicken breast
4 reduced-calorie whole wheat hamburger
    buns

Combine first 9 ingredients. Set aside ¼ cup tomato sauce mixture. Combine remaining tomato sauce mixture and chicken in an 11- x 7- x 1½-inch baking dish, stirring well. Cover and bake at 350° for 30 minutes or until thoroughly heated.

Spoon ½ cup chicken mixture onto bottom half of each bun; drizzle reserved ¼ cup tomato sauce mixture evenly over chicken mixture. Cover with bun tops. Yield: 4 servings.

PER SERVING: 268 CALORIES (13% FROM FAT)
FAT 3.8G (SATURATED FAT 1.3G)
PROTEIN 25.1G CARBOHYDRATE 31.9G
CHOLESTEROL 60MG SODIUM 446MG

Honey-Marinated Chicken Sandwich

HONEY-MARINATED CHICKEN SANDWICHES

⅓ cup low-sodium soy sauce
¼ cup honey
¼ cup unsweetened orange juice
¼ teaspoon garlic powder
¼ teaspoon ground ginger
1 pound chicken tenderloins
3 tablespoons plain nonfat yogurt
1 tablespoon reduced-calorie mayonnaise
1 tablespoon honey
1½ teaspoons Dijon mustard
1½ teaspoons coarse-grained mustard
Vegetable cooking spray
4 green leaf lettuce leaves
4 (¼-inch-thick) slices tomato
4 (¼-inch-thick) slices purple onion
4 (1½-ounce) sandwich rolls with sesame
   seeds, split and toasted

Combine first 5 ingredients, stirring with a wire whisk. Place chicken in a shallow dish; pour soy sauce mixture over chicken, turning to coat. Cover and marinate in refrigerator 30 minutes.

Combine yogurt and next 4 ingredients in a small bowl, stirring well; cover and set aside.

Remove chicken from marinade, reserving marinade. Place marinade in a small saucepan; bring to a boil. Remove from heat, and set aside.

Place chicken on rack of a broiler pan coated with cooking spray. Broil 5½ inches from heat (with electric oven door partially opened) 8 minutes or until done, turning and basting often with reserved marinade.

Arrange lettuce, tomato, and onion evenly on bottom halves of rolls. Arrange chicken evenly over onion. Spread yogurt mixture evenly over chicken. Cover with roll tops. Serve warm. Yield: 4 servings.

PER SERVING: 364 CALORIES (18% FROM FAT)
FAT 7.2G (SATURATED FAT 1.5G)
PROTEIN 32.2G   CARBOHYDRATE 40.9G
CHOLESTEROL 74MG   SODIUM 704MG

MONTE CRISTO LIGHT

¼ cup plus 2 tablespoons low-sugar
    strawberry spread
12 (1-ounce) slices Vienna or other sandwich
    bread
6 ounces thinly sliced cooked turkey breast
6 (¾-ounce) slices low-fat process Swiss
    cheese
2 eggs, lightly beaten
1 egg white, lightly beaten
½ cup skim milk
2 tablespoons yellow cornmeal
Butter-flavored vegetable cooking spray
1 tablespoon sifted powdered sugar

    Spread strawberry spread evenly on 1 side of
6 bread slices. Place turkey and cheese evenly
on strawberry spread; top with remaining 6 bread
slices.
    Combine eggs, egg white, and milk in a medium
bowl; stir well with a wire whisk. Carefully dip
sandwiches into egg mixture, allowing excess to
drip off. Sprinkle both sides of each sandwich
evenly with cornmeal.
    Coat a large nonstick skillet with cooking spray;
place over medium-low heat until hot. Place 3
sandwiches in skillet; cook 6 to 8 minutes on each
side or until bread is golden and cheese melts.
    Remove from skillet, and sprinkle evenly with
half of powdered sugar. Repeat procedure with
remaining 3 sandwiches and remaining powdered
sugar. Serve immediately. Yield: 6 servings.

PER SERVING: 314 CALORIES (14% FROM FAT)
FAT 4.9G (SATURATED FAT 0.9G)
PROTEIN 22.4G   CARBOHYDRATE 43.3G
CHOLESTEROL 94MG   SODIUM 635MG

HAM AND APPLE SANDWICHES

½ cup apple butter
2 teaspoons grated onion
½ teaspoon dry mustard
8 (1-ounce) slices raisin bread, toasted
¼ pound thinly sliced reduced-fat, low-salt
    ham
2 ounces Edam cheese, thinly sliced
1 small Red Delicious apple, cored and sliced
    crosswise into rings
Small apple wedges (optional)

    Combine first 3 ingredients, stirring well. Spread
evenly over 1 side of bread slices.
    Place ham, cheese, and apple rings evenly on
apple butter mixture on 4 bread slices. Top with
remaining bread slices, coated side down. Garnish
with apple wedges, if desired. Yield: 4 servings.

PER SERVING: 322 CALORIES (20% FROM FAT)
FAT 7.2G (SATURATED FAT 3.4G)
PROTEIN 12.6G   CARBOHYDRATE 53.7G
CHOLESTEROL 28MG   SODIUM 564MG

Menu Helper

    Take the boredom out of lunchtime by
using a variety of breads for your otherwise
basic sandwiches. French, Italian, and Vienna
breads make a fine sandwich as do bagels,
buns, pita bread, English muffins, whole
grain bread, or raisin bread. Most breads are
relatively low in fat and high in complex car-
bohydrates. See the nutrition information
labels for serving sizes and calories.

Ham and Apple Sandwich

Italian Tuna Submarine Sandwich

ITALIAN TUNA SUBMARINE SANDWICHES

2 medium-size sweet red peppers
2 tablespoons coarsely chopped sun-dried
     tomatoes (packed without salt or oil)
2 (6⅛-ounce) cans 60% less-salt tuna packed
     in spring water, drained
¼ cup plain nonfat yogurt
2 tablespoons thinly sliced green onions
1 tablespoon plus 1 teaspoon minced fresh
     basil
½ teaspoon cracked pepper
½ teaspoon hot sauce
4 romaine lettuce leaves
4 (2½-ounce) submarine rolls, split

Cut peppers in half lengthwise; remove and discard seeds and membrane. Place peppers, skin side
up, on a baking sheet; flatten with palm of hand.

Broil 5½ inches from heat (with electric oven door
partially opened) 15 to 20 minutes or until charred.
Place peppers in ice water, and chill 5 minutes.
Remove from water; peel and discard skins. Cut
peppers into julienne strips; set aside.

Place tomatoes in a small bowl; cover with hot
water, and let stand 15 minutes. Drain well; mince
tomatoes.

Combine tomato, tuna, and next 5 ingredients in
a medium bowl. Arrange lettuce leaves and red
pepper strips over bottom halves of rolls. Spread
tuna mixture evenly over peppers. Cover with roll
tops, and serve immediately. Yield: 4 servings.

PER SERVING: 299 CALORIES (9% FROM FAT)
FAT 2.9G (SATURATED FAT 0.6G)
PROTEIN 18.2G CARBOHYDRATE 49.6G
CHOLESTEROL 20MG SODIUM 588MG

INSIDE-OUT PIZZA

A pizza sandwich? Kids will love it! Toss a salad and slice some apples for quick side dishes.

1 cup bread flour
½ cup whole wheat flour
½ teaspoon sugar
¼ teaspoon salt
1 package active dry yeast
⅔ cup hot water (120° to 130°)
½ teaspoon olive oil
1 tablespoon bread flour
Vegetable cooking spray
4 ounces ultra-lean ground beef
1 cup chopped onion
1 clove garlic, minced
1 cup fat-free spaghetti sauce
⅛ teaspoon salt
½ cup (2 ounces) shredded part-skim
    mozzarella cheese

Combine first 5 ingredients in a large mixing bowl. Gradually add water and oil to flour mixture, beating well at low speed of an electric mixer. Beat 2 additional minutes at medium speed.

Sprinkle 1 tablespoon bread flour evenly over work surface. Turn dough out onto floured surface; knead until smooth and elastic (about 5 minutes). Place dough in a large bowl coated with cooking spray, turning to coat top. Cover and let rise in a warm place (85°), free from drafts, 1 hour or until doubled in bulk.

Punch dough down; turn out onto work surface. Knead lightly 4 or 5 times. Press onto a 12-inch pizza pan coated with cooking spray; set aside.

Coat a large nonstick skillet with cooking spray; place over medium-high heat until hot. Add ground beef, onion, and garlic. Cook until beef is browned, stirring until it crumbles; drain, if necessary, and return to skillet. Add spaghetti sauce and salt. Bring to a boil. Cover, reduce heat, and simmer 10 minutes, stirring occasionally.

Spoon meat mixture over half of dough in pizza pan, leaving a ½-inch border; sprinkle cheese over meat mixture. Moisten edge of dough with water. Fold uncoated half of dough over meat mixture to form a half circle; seal edges of dough by pressing firmly with a fork dipped in flour. Bake at 375° for 20 minutes or until golden. Cut pizza into 4 wedges. Serve warm. Yield: 4 servings.

PER SERVING: 306 CALORIES (17% FROM FAT)
FAT 5.8G (SATURATED FAT 2.4G)
PROTEIN 16.8G CARBOHYDRATE 47.6G
CHOLESTEROL 26MG SODIUM 523MG

MEDITERRANEAN PITA PIZZAS

Vegetable cooking spray
6 ounces lean ground lamb
2½ cups peeled, cubed eggplant (about ½
    pound)
⅓ cup water
½ teaspoon dried oregano
½ teaspoon lemon juice
¼ teaspoon garlic powder
⅓ cup Italian-style tomato paste
2 (8-inch) pita bread rounds, toasted
3 tablespoons crumbled feta cheese

Coat a large skillet with cooking spray; place over medium-high heat until hot. Add ground lamb; cook until meat is browned, stirring until it crumbles. Drain and set aside. Wipe drippings from skillet with a paper towel.

Add eggplant to skillet; cook over medium-high heat, stirring constantly, 2 minutes. Add water and next 3 ingredients to skillet; stir well. Cover, reduce heat, and cook 5 minutes. Uncover and cook over high heat 1 additional minute. Add lamb and tomato paste; cook until thoroughly heated, stirring occasionally.

Place pita rounds on a baking sheet. Spread lamb mixture evenly over pita rounds, and top with cheese. Broil 5½ inches from heat (with electric oven door partially opened) 2 minutes or until cheese softens. Yield: 2 servings.

PER SERVING: 386 CALORIES (25% FROM FAT)
FAT 10.7G (SATURATED FAT 4.2G)
PROTEIN 25.5G CARBOHYDRATE 45.6G
CHOLESTEROL 68MG SODIUM 456MG

Country Chicken Pot Pie (recipe on page 62)

EVENING ENTRÉES

Do you remember favorite meals from your childhood that you would like to share with your own family? Here are some of those tried-and-true recipes but with one major difference—they have been modified for today's healthier low-fat way of eating.

Who would imagine that recipes like Mama's Meat Loaf and Pennsylvania Pot Roast (page 55), Ham and Lima Bean Casserole (page 59), and Creamy Four-Cheese Macaroni (page 70) could be so low in fat and calories? The recipe titles in this chapter may sound like those your grandmother prepared, but there the similarity stops. Thanks to careful ingredient selection and improved cooking methods, calories from fat in these dishes are now less than 30 percent.

You can turn to any one of the following pages to find recipes for some of the best food around.

Slow-Cooker Beef and Bean Burritos

SLOW-COOKER BEEF AND BEAN BURRITOS

1 (2-pound) London broil
1 (1.25-ounce) package taco seasoning mix
Vegetable cooking spray
1 cup chopped onion
1 tablespoon white vinegar
1 (4.5-ounce) can chopped green chiles,
    undrained
1 (16-ounce) can fat-free refried beans
12 (8-inch) fat-free flour tortillas
1½ cups (6 ounces) shredded Monterey Jack
    cheese
1½ cups chopped plum tomato
¾ cup nonfat sour cream

Trim fat from meat; rub seasoning mix over both sides of meat. Place meat in an electric slow cooker coated with cooking spray; add onion, vinegar, and green chiles. Cover and cook on low-heat setting 9 hours. Remove meat from slow cooker, reserving cooking liquid; shred meat with two forks. Combine shredded meat and reserved cooking liquid; stir mixture well.

Heat beans and tortillas according to package directions. Spread 2 tablespoons beans down center of each tortilla. Spoon a heaping ⅓ cup meat mixture on top of beans. Top each with 2 tablespoons cheese, 2 tablespoons tomato, and 1 tablespoon sour cream; roll up. Yield: 12 servings.

PER SERVING: 350 CALORIES (30% FROM FAT)
FAT 11.8G (SATURATED FAT 6.1G)
PROTEIN 24.0G   CARBOHYDRATE 31.3G
CHOLESTEROL 49MG   SODIUM 839MG

PENNSYLVANIA POT ROAST

(pictured on cover)

This old-fashioned pot roast is the very essence of comfort food.

1 (3-pound) beef eye of round roast
Vegetable cooking spray
1 cup canned beef broth, undiluted
2 cups chopped onion
½ cup canned crushed tomatoes with added
    puree, undrained
½ cup chopped carrot
½ cup chopped celery
½ cup chopped turnips
3 tablespoons chopped fresh parsley
½ teaspoon dried thyme
¼ teaspoon coarsely ground black pepper
2 bay leaves
10 small new potatoes, cut in half
5 small carrots, scraped and cut diagonally
    into 2-inch pieces
3 small onions, each quartered
Fresh thyme leaves (optional)
Fresh bay leaves (optional)

Trim fat from roast. Coat a Dutch oven with cooking spray; place over medium-high heat until hot. Add roast; cook until browned on all sides. Add broth and next 9 ingredients to Dutch oven; bring to a boil. Cover, reduce heat, and simmer 1 hour. Add potato halves, 5 carrots, and 3 onions. Cover and cook 25 minutes or until meat and vegetables are tender.

Transfer roast to a serving platter. Cut diagonally across grain into thin slices. Arrange larger vegetable pieces around roast. Set aside; keep warm.

Cook broth mixture in Dutch oven, uncovered, over medium heat 10 minutes. Remove and discard bay leaves. Serve sauce with roast. If desired, garnish with fresh thyme and fresh bay leaves. Yield: 10 servings.

PER SERVING: 260 CALORIES (20% FROM FAT)
FAT 5.8G (SATURATED FAT 2.0G)
PROTEIN 34.2G   CARBOHYDRATE 16.7G
CHOLESTEROL 82MG   SODIUM 271MG

MAMA'S MEAT LOAF

1 cup chopped onion
1 cup chopped green pepper
3 tablespoons minced fresh parsley
1 teaspoon pepper
¾ teaspoon salt
2 cloves garlic, minced
1 egg, lightly beaten
1 (1-ounce) slice white bread, torn into small
    pieces
1½ pounds ground round
Vegetable cooking spray
⅓ cup ketchup

Combine first 8 ingredients in a large bowl, tossing to moisten bread. Crumble meat over onion mixture, and stir just until blended. Pack mixture into a 9- x 5- x 3-inch loafpan coated with cooking spray. Spread ketchup over loaf.

Bake at 350° for 1 hour or until a meat thermometer registers 160°. Let stand in pan 10 minutes. Remove from pan; cut into 6 slices. Yield: 6 servings.

Note: Serve leftover slices on whole wheat bread with mayonnaise, lettuce, and Cheddar cheese.

PER SERVING: 220 CALORIES (28% FROM FAT)
FAT 6.9G (SATURATED FAT 2.4G)
PROTEIN 27.4G   CARBOHYDRATE 10.8G
CHOLESTEROL 101MG   SODIUM 552MG

Exercise Tricks

Exercise doesn't have to be all work and no play—just use your imagination to make it enjoyable.

• Vary the exercise to avoid getting bored.

• Remember the long-term benefits of exercise, such as having more energy and achieving better health.

• If the exercise isn't interesting, distract yourself with something that is.

• Exercise together as a family or with a friend. Besides having a chance to visit, you will be motivated to keep a commitment.

Chili Mac

CHILI MAC

1 pound ground round
½ cup chopped onion
½ cup chopped green pepper
3 cloves garlic, minced
2 cups cooked elbow macaroni (cooked
    without salt or fat)
½ cup water
1 tablespoon chili powder
1 teaspoon ground cumin
½ teaspoon salt
¼ teaspoon pepper
1 (15¼-ounce) can kidney beans, drained
1 (14½-ounce) can no-salt-added whole
    tomatoes, undrained and chopped
1 (8¾-ounce) can no-salt-added whole-kernel
    corn, drained
1 (8-ounce) can no-salt-added tomato sauce
1 (6-ounce) can no-salt-added tomato paste
1 cup (4 ounces) shredded reduced-fat sharp
    Cheddar cheese

Cook first 4 ingredients in a Dutch oven over
medium-high heat until meat is browned, stirring
until meat crumbles. Drain well; wipe drippings
from Dutch oven with a paper towel. Return beef
mixture to Dutch oven.

Add macaroni and next 10 ingredients to beef
mixture, stirring well. Bring mixture to a boil;
cover, reduce heat, and simmer 20 minutes,
stirring occasionally. Spoon evenly into eight
individual serving bowls, and sprinkle 2 tablespoons cheese over each serving. Yield: 8 (1-cup)
servings.

PER SERVING: 309 CALORIES (21% FROM FAT)
FAT 7.2G (SATURATED FAT 2.9G)
PROTEIN 25.1G   CARBOHYDRATE 36.9G
CHOLESTEROL 44MG   SODIUM 420MG

VEAL PARMESAN WITH TOMATO SALSA

8 (6-ounce) lean veal loin chops (¾ inch thick)
1 cup crushed toasted whole grain wheat flake cereal
¼ cup grated Parmesan cheese
2 egg whites, lightly beaten
Vegetable cooking spray
2 cups peeled, seeded, and chopped plum tomato
1 cup thinly sliced arugula
½ cup sliced green onions
2 tablespoons minced fresh basil
2 tablespoons red wine vinegar
1 tablespoon olive oil
¼ teaspoon garlic powder
¼ teaspoon pepper
½ cup (2 ounces) shredded part-skim mozzarella cheese

Trim fat from veal. Combine crushed cereal and Parmesan cheese in a shallow bowl. Dip veal in egg whites, and dredge in cereal mixture. Place veal in a 13- x 9- x 2-inch baking dish coated with cooking spray. Cover and chill 1 hour.

Combine tomato and next 7 ingredients in a small bowl. Cover and set aside.

Bake veal, uncovered, at 375° for 30 to 35 minutes or until tender. Sprinkle with mozzarella cheese; bake 5 additional minutes or until cheese melts. Transfer to a serving platter, and spoon tomato mixture evenly over veal. Yield: 8 servings.

PER SERVING: 251 CALORIES (28% FROM FAT)
FAT 7.8G (SATURATED FAT 2.6G)
PROTEIN 28.5G CARBOHYDRATE 16.8G
CHOLESTEROL 97MG SODIUM 310MG

PORK MEDALLIONS WITH GLAZED APPLES

Cooked apples are a popular addition to savory pork dishes. To get the best flavor, use a tart, slightly acidic apple such as Granny Smith or Newtown pippin. However, any good, all-purpose cooking apple will do.

Vegetable cooking spray
1 teaspoon vegetable oil
1 (1-pound) pork tenderloin, cut into ¼-inch-thick slices
2 large Granny Smith apples, peeled, cored, and cut into ¼-inch-thick rings
⅓ cup frozen unsweetened apple juice concentrate, thawed and undiluted
2 teaspoons Dijon mustard
¼ teaspoon salt
¼ teaspoon pepper

Coat a large nonstick skillet with cooking spray; add oil. Place over medium-high heat until hot. Add pork, and cook until browned on both sides, turning once. Drain and pat dry with paper towels. Set pork aside.

Coat skillet with cooking spray, and place over medium-high heat until hot. Add apple rings; sauté until tender. Add apple juice concentrate, and bring to a boil. Stir in mustard, salt, and pepper; add pork. Cook until thoroughly heated. Serve immediately. Yield: 4 servings.

PER SERVING: 220 CALORIES (24% FROM FAT)
FAT 5.9G (SATURATED FAT 1.7G)
PROTEIN 24.7G CARBOHYDRATE 16.7G
CHOLESTEROL 79MG SODIUM 278MG

PORK CHOPS WITH CHUNKY TOMATO SAUCE

Keep a jar of pickled jalapeño peppers on hand for this recipe and to use as a substitute for fresh jalapeños in other recipes.

1 teaspoon ground cumin
1 teaspoon chili powder
2 teaspoons cider vinegar
½ teaspoon ground cinnamon
4 (6-ounce) lean center-cut pork chops (about ¾ inch thick)
1 teaspoon vegetable oil
1½ cups chopped sweet red pepper
½ cup chopped green onions
2 tablespoons finely chopped pickled jalapeño pepper
1 tablespoon plus 1 teaspoon minced garlic
1 (16-ounce) package frozen whole-kernel corn, thawed
1 teaspoon dried oregano
1 (14.5-ounce) can diced tomatoes, drained
Fresh parsley sprigs (optional)

Combine first 4 ingredients; stir well. Rub over both sides of pork.

Heat oil in a large nonstick skillet over medium-high heat until hot. Add pork; cook 3 minutes on each side or until browned. Add red pepper and next 6 ingredients, scraping bottom of skillet to loosen browned bits.

Cover, reduce heat, and simmer 45 minutes or until pork is tender. Garnish with fresh parsley sprigs, if desired. Yield: 4 servings.

PER SERVING: 325 CALORIES (28% FROM FAT)
FAT 10.0G (SATURATED FAT 3.1G)
PROTEIN 30.1G CARBOHYDRATE 32.2G
CHOLESTEROL 71MG SODIUM 179MG

MAPLE-GLAZED HAM WITH MAPLE-MUSTARD SAUCE

1 (8½-pound) 33%-less-sodium smoked, fully cooked ham half
Vegetable cooking spray
1¼ cups maple syrup, divided
⅔ cup Dijon mustard, divided
1 teaspoon grated orange rind
2 tablespoons unsweetened orange juice
1 cup orange marmalade

Trim fat and rind from ham. Make shallow cuts in ham in a diamond pattern. Place ham on a rack coated with cooking spray; place rack in a shallow roasting pan.

Combine ¼ cup maple syrup, 2 tablespoons mustard, orange rind, and orange juice; stir well, and brush over ham. Bake at 425° for 5 minutes. Reduce oven temperature to 325°, and cook 1 hour and 30 minutes or until thoroughly heated. Baste ham with maple syrup mixture every 30 minutes. Transfer ham to a platter, and let stand 15 minutes before slicing.

Combine remaining 1 cup syrup, remaining ½ cup plus 2 teaspoons mustard, and marmalade in a small saucepan. Cook, stirring constantly, over medium heat 3 minutes or until thoroughly heated. Serve sauce with ham. Yield: 24 servings.

PER SERVING: 177 CALORIES (23% FROM FAT)
FAT 4.6G (SATURATED FAT 1.5G)
PROTEIN 15.3G CARBOHYDRATE 19.4G
CHOLESTEROL 42MG SODIUM 845MG

HAM AND LIMA BEAN CASSEROLE

1½ cups water
1½ cups frozen baby lima beans, thawed
¾ cup finely chopped green pepper
⅓ cup chopped onion
1¼ cups chopped extra-lean ham (about 6 ounces)
1 cup (4 ounces) shredded reduced-fat sharp Cheddar cheese
1 teaspoon Worcestershire sauce
1 (14¾-ounce) can no-salt-added cream-style corn
Vegetable cooking spray
¼ cup plus 2 tablespoons skim milk
2 tablespoons chopped green onions
¾ cup low-fat biscuit and baking mix

Bring water to a boil in a medium saucepan. Add lima beans, pepper, and ⅓ cup onion; cover and cook 5 minutes. Drain. Combine lima bean mixture, ham, and next 3 ingredients; stir well. Spoon into a 2-quart casserole coated with cooking spray. Cover and bake at 400° for 20 minutes.

Combine milk and green onions in a bowl, and stir in baking mix. Drop batter by spoonfuls onto ham mixture to form 6 biscuits. Bake, uncovered, 20 minutes or until biscuits are golden. Spoon mixture into six serving bowls, and top each with 1 biscuit. Yield: 6 servings.

Note: You can also assemble the casserole ahead of time, omitting the biscuit topping; cover casserole, and chill or freeze. Thaw frozen casserole overnight in refrigerator. Let stand at room temperature 30 minutes. Add biscuit topping; bake as directed.

PER SERVING: 317 CALORIES (18% FROM FAT)
FAT 6.2G (SATURATED FAT 2.7G)
PROTEIN 19.8G   CARBOHYDRATE 70.7G
CHOLESTEROL 28MG   SODIUM 846MG

Ham and Lima Bean Casserole

CHICKEN AND RICE WITH CREAMY HERB SAUCE

¾ cup water
¼ cup dry white wine
1 teaspoon chicken-flavored bouillon granules
4 (4-ounce) skinned, boned chicken breast halves
1 tablespoon water
½ teaspoon cornstarch
¼ cup plus 1 tablespoon tub-style light cream cheese with garlic and spices
4 cups hot cooked long-grain rice (cooked without salt or fat)
Chopped fresh parsley

Bring first 3 ingredients to a boil in a large skillet; add chicken. Cover, reduce heat, and simmer 15 minutes, turning chicken after 8 minutes. Remove chicken from skillet, reserving liquid in skillet. Set aside, and keep warm.

Bring cooking liquid to a boil; cook, uncovered, 5 minutes or until reduced to ⅔ cup. Combine 1 tablespoon water and cornstarch; add to skillet. Bring to a boil; cook, stirring constantly, 1 minute. Add cream cheese; cook, stirring constantly with a wire whisk, until well blended. Serve each chicken breast half over 1 cup rice; top each with 3 table-spoons sauce and parsley. Yield: 4 servings.

PER SERVING: 399 CALORIES (12% FROM FAT)
FAT 5.5G (SATURATED FAT 2.6G)
PROTEIN 32.7G   CARBOHYDRATE 51.6G
CHOLESTEROL 78MG   SODIUM 400MG

EASY SLOW-COOKER CHICKEN

Slow cookers are wonderful because you can just combine everything in one pot and let it cook.

6 chicken drumsticks (about 1½ pounds), skinned
6 chicken thighs (about 3 pounds), skinned
⅓ cup dry white wine or no-salt-added chicken broth
¼ cup instant chopped onion
2 teaspoons chicken-flavored bouillon granules
½ teaspoon dried Italian seasoning
½ teaspoon salt-free lemon-herb seasoning
¼ teaspoon garlic powder
¼ teaspoon dried tarragon
¼ teaspoon dried crushed red pepper
1 (14.5-ounce) can no-salt-added stewed tomatoes, undrained and chopped
4½ cups hot cooked rice (cooked without salt or fat)

Trim fat from chicken. Place chicken in an electric slow cooker; stir in wine and next 8 ingredients. Cover and cook on high-heat setting 1 hour. Reduce heat setting to low, and cook 3½ hours. For each serving, place 1 chicken drumstick and 1 chicken thigh over ¾ cup rice; top each serving with ½ cup sauce. Yield: 6 servings.

PER SERVING: 460 CALORIES (17% FROM FAT)
FAT 8.8G (SATURATED FAT 2.2G)
PROTEIN 47.8G   CARBOHYDRATE 44.3G
CHOLESTEROL 177MG   SODIUM 506MG

Kids in the Kitchen

The kids are in the kitchen, eager to help—but what can their little hands do? Pull out your slow cooker. The children can help measure and add ingredients. For the slow-cooker recipe above, they can even use kitchen scissors to cut up tomatoes right in the can. And all the ingredients are added before turning on the cooker, so you needn't worry about young children getting burned. A word of caution: once you turn on the slow cooker, be sure to push it toward the back of the counter. The outside will become hot during cooking and could burn those curious fingers. (Turn to page 7 for more about slow cookers.)

COMPANY CHICKEN AND RICE CASSEROLE

1 (6.9-ounce) package one-third-less-salt
  chicken-flavored rice-and-vermicelli mix
  with chicken broth and herbs
1 tablespoon margarine
2¼ cups hot water
Vegetable cooking spray
1½ pounds skinned, boned chicken breast
  halves, cut into bite-size pieces
1 cup sliced fresh mushrooms
½ teaspoon garlic powder
¾ cup nonfat sour cream
¼ teaspoon pepper
1 (10¾-ounce) can reduced-fat,
  reduced-sodium cream of mushroom
  soup, undiluted
¼ cup crushed multigrain crackers (about
  6 crackers)
1 tablespoon margarine, melted
½ teaspoon poppy seeds

Cook rice in a large nonstick skillet according to package directions, using 1 tablespoon margarine and 2¼ cups hot water. Remove from skillet; set aside. Wipe skillet with a paper towel.

Coat skillet with cooking spray; place over high heat until hot. Add chicken, mushrooms, and garlic powder; sauté 6 minutes or until chicken is done.

Combine rice mixture, chicken mixture, sour cream, pepper, and soup; stir well. Spoon into a 2-quart casserole coated with cooking spray.

Combine cracker crumbs, melted margarine, and poppy seeds; stir well, and sprinkle over casserole. Bake, uncovered, at 350° for 35 minutes or until thoroughly heated. Yield: 6 (1⅓-cup) servings.

Note: If desired, assemble this casserole ahead, omitting the cracker-crumb mixture; cover casserole, and chill or freeze. Thaw frozen casserole overnight in refrigerator. Let stand at room temperature 30 minutes. Top with cracker-crumb mixture, and bake as directed.

PER SERVING: 334 CALORIES (18% FROM FAT)
FAT 6.8G (SATURATED FAT 1.6G)
PROTEIN 32.2G CARBOHYDRATE 30.0G
CHOLESTEROL 68MG SODIUM 687MG

CHICKEN AND NOODLES

*A rich, flavorful vegetable puree thickens the broth
without adding fat.*

1 (3-pound) broiler-fryer, cut up and skinned
7 cups water
½ cup chopped fresh parsley
6 cloves garlic
2 medium carrots, scraped and cut into
  1-inch pieces
2 medium parsnips, scraped and cut into
  1-inch pieces
2 stalks celery, cut into 1-inch pieces
2 medium turnips, peeled and quartered
1 large onion, sliced
1 bay leaf
12 ounces medium egg noodles, uncooked
½ teaspoon salt
½ teaspoon pepper

Combine first 10 ingredients in a Dutch oven. Bring to a boil; cover, reduce heat, and simmer 2½ hours. Remove chicken, vegetables, and bay leaf from broth, reserving broth; discard bay leaf. Bone and coarsely chop chicken; set aside.

Position knife blade in food processor bowl; add vegetable mixture. Process until smooth, scraping sides of processor bowl once; set aside.

Skim fat from broth. Add chicken to broth in Dutch oven; bring to a boil. Stir in noodles; reduce heat, and simmer, uncovered, 8 minutes or until noodles are tender. Stir in vegetable puree, salt, and pepper. Cook until thoroughly heated. Yield: 10 (1-cup) servings.

PER SERVING: 277 CALORIES (18% FROM FAT)
FAT 5.5G (SATURATED FAT 1.4G)
PROTEIN 21.3G CARBOHYDRATE 32.7G
CHOLESTEROL 80MG SODIUM 202MG

COUNTRY CHICKEN POT PIE

(pictured on page 52)

2 pounds skinned chicken breast halves
4 sprigs fresh parsley
3 stalks celery, cut into 2-inch pieces
1 small onion, quartered
1 bay leaf
5 cups water
Vegetable cooking spray
1 cup chopped onion
¾ cup diced celery
1½ cups peeled, cubed potato
1 (10-ounce) package frozen mixed vegetables
⅔ cup all-purpose flour
1 (12-ounce) can evaporated skimmed milk, divided
½ teaspoon salt
½ teaspoon poultry seasoning
¼ teaspoon pepper
¼ teaspoon dried thyme
2 cups low-fat biscuit and baking mix
2 tablespoons chopped fresh parsley
¾ cup 1% low-fat milk

Combine first 6 ingredients in a Dutch oven. Bring to a boil; cover, reduce heat, and simmer 1 hour. Remove chicken from broth, reserving broth. Let chicken cool. Bone and coarsely chop chicken; set aside. Pour broth through a wire-mesh strainer lined with a layer of cheesecloth into a bowl, discarding vegetables and herbs remaining in strainer. Skim fat from broth, and set aside 4 cups broth. Reserve remaining broth for another use.

Coat Dutch oven with cooking spray; place over medium-high heat until hot. Add chopped onion and celery; sauté until tender. Add reserved 4 cups broth, potato, and frozen mixed vegetables; bring to a boil. Cover, reduce heat, and simmer 15 minutes or until vegetables are tender.

Combine flour and ¾ cup evaporated milk in a small bowl, stirring until smooth. Add to vegetable mixture in Dutch oven, stirring constantly. Add remaining evaporated milk; cook over medium heat, stirring constantly, until mixture is thickened and bubbly. Remove from heat. Stir in chopped chicken, salt, and next 3 ingredients. Spoon into a 13- x 9- x 2-inch baking dish coated with cooking spray.

Combine baking mix and chopped parsley. Add low-fat milk, stirring just until moistened. Drop dough by heaping spoonfuls onto chicken mixture to form 8 biscuits. Bake, uncovered, at 350° for 35 minutes or until golden. Yield: 8 servings.

Note: For a lower-sodium biscuit topping, replace low-fat biscuit and baking mix with 2 cups all-purpose flour, 2 teaspoons baking powder, and ½ teaspoon salt; add 2 tablespoons parsley. Add ½ tablespoons melted margarine and ¾ cup low-fat milk to dry ingredients, stirring just until moistened.

PER SERVING: 384 CALORIES (8% FROM FAT)
FAT 3.4G (SATURATED FAT 0.9G)
PROTEIN 29.1G CARBOHYDRATE 64.6G
CHOLESTEROL 55MG SODIUM 796MG

CHICKEN AND HAM TETRAZZINI

1 (7-ounce) package spaghetti, uncooked
1 tablespoon reduced-calorie margarine
1 cup sliced fresh mushrooms
1 cup chopped onion
1 cup chopped green pepper
2 cloves garlic, minced
¼ cup all-purpose flour
½ teaspoon poultry seasoning
½ teaspoon pepper
1¼ cups 1% low-fat milk
¾ cup (3 ounces) shredded reduced-fat sharp Cheddar cheese, divided
1½ cups skinned, shredded roasted chicken breast (about 5 ounces)
¾ cup finely chopped cooked extra-lean ham (about ¼ pound)
⅔ cup grated Parmesan cheese, divided
¼ cup dry sherry
1 (10¾-ounce) can reduced-fat, reduced-sodium cream of mushroom soup
1 (4-ounce) jar diced pimiento, drained
Vegetable cooking spray
1 teaspoon paprika
2 tablespoons sliced almonds

Chicken and Ham Tetrazzini

Cook pasta according to package directions, omitting salt and fat; drain well. Rinse under cold running water; drain well, and set aside.

Melt margarine in a nonstick skillet over medium-high heat. Add mushrooms and next 3 ingredients; sauté 4 minutes or until tender. Stir in flour, poultry seasoning, and ½ teaspoon pepper; cook, stirring constantly, 30 seconds. Add milk; cook, stirring constantly, 1½ minutes or until thickened. Remove from heat; stir in ¼ cup Cheddar cheese, stirring until cheese melts. Add chicken, ham, ⅓ cup Parmesan, and next 3 ingredients; stir well.

Combine pasta and chicken mixture in a large bowl; stir well. Spoon mixture into a 13- x 9- x 2-inch baking dish coated with cooking spray.

Combine remaining ⅓ cup Parmesan cheese and paprika, and stir well. Sprinkle Parmesan cheese mixture, remaining ½ cup Cheddar cheese, and almonds in alternating diagonal rows over casserole.

Bake casserole, uncovered, at 350° for 20 minutes or until bubbly. Yield: 6 (2-cup) servings.

Note: To assemble casserole up to 4 hours ahead, omit cheese-almond topping; cover and chill. Add topping just before baking.

PER SERVING: 397 CALORIES (26% FROM FAT)
FAT 11.6G (SATURATED FAT 4.8G)
PROTEIN 27.5G CARBOHYDRATE 42.2G
CHOLESTEROL 51MG SODIUM 775MG

PASTA CARBONARA

6 ounces turkey bacon, chopped
2 cloves garlic, minced
6 cups hot cooked thin spaghetti (about 12
    ounces uncooked pasta), cooked without
    salt or fat
¼ cup grated Parmesan cheese
2 tablespoons minced fresh parsley
¼ teaspoon freshly ground pepper
1 cup 2% low-fat milk
¼ cup plus 2 tablespoons fat-free egg
    substitute

Cook bacon in a large nonstick skillet over medium-high heat until crisp. Add garlic; sauté 1 minute or until tender. Reduce heat to low; stir in pasta and next 3 ingredients. Combine milk and egg substitute; stir well. Add to skillet; cook, stirring constantly, 3 minutes or until sauce thickens. Serve immediately. Yield: 6 (1-cup) servings.

PER SERVING: 284 CALORIES (19% FROM FAT)
FAT 6.1G (SATURATED FAT 2.1G)
PROTEIN 14.4G   CARBOHYDRATE 44.1G
CHOLESTEROL 23MG   SODIUM 441MG

Pasta Carbonara

CHILES RELLENOS CASSEROLE

½ pound ground turkey or chicken
1 cup chopped onion
1¾ teaspoons ground cumin
1½ teaspoons dried oregano
½ teaspoon garlic powder
¼ teaspoon salt
¼ teaspoon pepper
1 (16-ounce) can fat-free refried beans
2 (4-ounce) cans whole green chiles, drained,
    cut lengthwise into quarters, and divided
Vegetable cooking spray
1 cup (4 ounces) shredded colby-Monterey
    Jack cheese blend, divided
1 cup frozen whole-kernel corn, thawed and
    drained
⅓ cup all-purpose flour
¼ teaspoon salt
1⅓ cups skim milk
⅛ teaspoon hot sauce
2 eggs, lightly beaten
2 egg whites

Cook turkey and onion in a large nonstick skillet over medium-high heat until turkey is browned, stirring until it crumbles. Remove from heat; add cumin and next 5 ingredients to turkey mixture. Stir well, and set aside.

Arrange half of green chile quarters in an 11- x 7- x 1½-inch baking dish coated with cooking spray; top with half of cheese. Spoon turkey mixture in mounds onto cheese, and spread gently, leaving a ¼-inch border around edge of dish; top with corn. Arrange remaining chile quarters over corn; top with remaining cheese. Set aside.

Combine flour and ¼ teaspoon salt in a medium bowl; gradually add milk and hot sauce, stirring with a wire whisk until blended. Stir in eggs and egg whites; pour over casserole. Bake, uncovered, at 350° for 1 hour and 5 minutes or until set; let stand 5 minutes. Cut into squares to serve. Yield: 6 servings.

PER SERVING: 340 CALORIES (26% FROM FAT)
FAT 9.8G (SATURATED FAT 4.8G)
PROTEIN 26.1G CARBOHYDRATE 38.0G
CHOLESTEROL 117MG SODIUM 890MG

BAKED SNAPPER VERACRUZANA

This spicy dish gets its name from the state of Veracruz on the eastern coast of Mexico.

Vegetable cooking spray
1½ cups thinly sliced onion
2 tablespoons minced fresh garlic
1 cup thinly sliced sweet red pepper
½ cup thinly sliced celery
¼ cup sliced pimiento-stuffed olives
2 tablespoons seeded, minced jalapeño pepper
1 tablespoon capers, drained
2 (14.5-ounce) cans no-salt-added stewed
    tomatoes, drained
¼ teaspoon fennel seeds
6 (4-ounce) red snapper fillets

Coat a large nonstick skillet with cooking spray; place over medium-high heat until hot. Add onion and garlic; sauté 5 minutes or just until tender. Add red pepper and next 4 ingredients; cook 10 minutes, stirring often. Add tomatoes and fennel seeds; cook, uncovered, 15 minutes.

Place fish in a 13- x 9- x 2-inch baking dish coated with cooking spray. Spoon vegetable mixture evenly over fish. Bake at 400° for 15 minutes or until fish flakes easily when tested with a fork. Yield: 6 servings.

PER SERVING: 186 CALORIES (11% FROM FAT)
FAT 2.3G (SATURATED FAT 0.4G)
PROTEIN 25.9G CARBOHYDRATE 15.7G
CHOLESTEROL 42MG SODIUM 287MG

TUNA ROMANOFF

Vegetable cooking spray
1 cup sliced fresh mushrooms
1 cup chopped onion
⅓ cup sliced celery
1 small clove garlic, minced
¾ cup 1% low-fat milk
¼ cup grated Parmesan cheese
¼ cup reduced-calorie mayonnaise
½ teaspoon dried dillweed
¼ teaspoon salt
¼ teaspoon pepper
1 (10¾-ounce) can reduced-fat,
    reduced-sodium condensed cream of
    celery soup, undiluted
3½ cups cooked medium egg noodles (about
    2¼ cups uncooked), cooked without salt
    or fat
1 cup frozen English peas
1 (9¼-ounce) can tuna in water, drained and
    flaked
1 (2-ounce) jar diced pimiento, drained
¼ cup dry breadcrumbs
¼ cup grated Parmesan cheese
1 tablespoon margarine, melted

Coat a large nonstick skillet with cooking spray;
place over medium heat until hot. Add mushrooms
and next 3 ingredients; sauté 6 minutes or until
tender. Combine milk and next 6 ingredients in
a large bowl; stir well. Add mushroom mixture,
noodles, and next 3 ingredients; stir gently.

Spoon noodle mixture into a shallow 2-quart
casserole coated with cooking spray. Cover and
bake at 350° for 40 minutes.

Combine breadcrumbs, ¼ cup Parmesan cheese,
and margarine in a small bowl; stir well. Sprinkle
over casserole. Bake, uncovered, at 350° for 10 minutes. Yield: 6 (1-cup) servings.

Note: You can assemble casserole up to 4 hours
ahead, omitting breadcrumb mixture; cover and
chill. Let stand at room temperature 30 minutes.
Add breadcrumb mixture, and bake as directed.

PER SERVING: 336 CALORIES (28% FROM FAT)
FAT 10.5G (SATURATED FAT 2.8G)
PROTEIN 20.1G   CARBOHYDRATE 39.6G
CHOLESTEROL 57MG   SODIUM 741MG

CRISPY FISH STICKS

3 (1-ounce) slices French bread, cubed
3 tablespoons reduced-fat mayonnaise
2 teaspoons water
½ teaspoon grated lemon rind
1 teaspoon lemon juice
1½ pounds grouper or other firm white fish
    fillets, cut into 1-inch-wide strips
Vegetable cooking spray

Position knife blade in food processor bowl; add
bread cubes. Process 30 seconds or until crumbs
are fine. Sprinkle breadcrumbs on an ungreased
baking sheet; bake at 350° for 12 minutes or until
browned. Set aside.

Combine mayonnaise and next 3 ingredients in a
shallow bowl; stir well. Dip fish in mayonnaise mixture, and dredge in breadcrumbs. Place fish on a
baking sheet coated with cooking spray. Bake at
425° for 22 to 25 minutes or until crispy and
browned. Yield: 6 servings.

PER SERVING: 167 CALORIES (19% FROM FAT)
FAT 3.6G (SATURATED FAT 0.5G)
PROTEIN 23.3G   CARBOHYDRATE 8.4G
CHOLESTEROL 45MG   SODIUM 198MG

Menu Helper

When you prepare the easy recipe for
Crispy Fish Sticks, keep the menu simple by
serving new potatoes and coleslaw on the side.
Simply boil the potatoes until tender; then
toss them with a small amount of reduced-
calorie margarine and freshly ground pepper.
For the slaw, start with preshredded cabbage;
add reduced-calorie coleslaw dressing, or
make your own dressing with reduced-calorie
mayonnaise and seasonings.

Crispy Fish Sticks

Lime-Marinated Shrimp Kabobs

LIME-MARINATED SHRIMP KABOBS

Mesquite wood chips impart a smoky, slightly sweet flavor to the grilled shrimp.

½ cup mesquite wood chips or other seasoned wood chips
2 pounds unpeeled large fresh shrimp
¼ cup lime juice
3 tablespoons chopped fresh parsley
2 tablespoons low-sodium soy sauce
1 tablespoon olive oil
3 cloves garlic, minced
Vegetable cooking spray
Lime wedges (optional)
Orange curls (optional)

Soak wood chips in water to cover 30 minutes; drain chips.

Peel and devein shrimp, leaving tails intact.

Combine lime juice and next 4 ingredients in a shallow dish; stir well. Add shrimp, tossing to coat. Cover and chill 30 minutes. Drain shrimp, reserving marinade. Thread shrimp onto six 12-inch skewers. Brush kabobs with reserved marinade.

Place wood chips over coals. Coat grill rack with cooking spray; place on grill over medium-hot coals (350° to 400°). Place kabobs on rack; grill, covered, 3 to 4 minutes. Turn kabobs, and brush with marinade. Grill, covered, 3 to 4 additional minutes or until shrimp turn pink. (Do not overcook.) If desired, garnish with lime wedges and orange curls. Yield: 6 servings.

PER SERVING: 113 CALORIES (26% FROM FAT)
FAT 3.3G (SATURATED FAT 0.6G)
PROTEIN 18.0G CARBOHYDRATE 1.5G
CHOLESTEROL 166MG SODIUM 322MG

SHRIMP AU GRATIN

1¼ pounds unpeeled medium-size fresh shrimp
Vegetable cooking spray
3 tablespoons reduced-calorie margarine, divided
⅓ cup chopped sweet red pepper
⅓ cup chopped green pepper
¼ cup chopped onion
2 cloves garlic, minced
2 tablespoons all-purpose flour
1½ cups skim milk
1 cup cooked rice (cooked without salt or fat)
1½ tablespoons fresh lemon juice
⅛ teaspoon pepper
½ cup soft whole wheat breadcrumbs
1 tablespoon grated Parmesan cheese
1 tablespoon minced fresh parsley

Peel and devein shrimp. Coat a large nonstick skillet with cooking spray; add 2 teaspoons margarine, and place over medium-high heat until margarine melts. Add shrimp, chopped red pepper, and next 3 ingredients; sauté 3 minutes. Remove from skillet, and set aside.

Melt remaining 2 tablespoons plus 1 teaspoon margarine in skillet over medium-low heat; add flour. Cook 1 minute, stirring constantly with a wire whisk. Gradually add milk. Cook, stirring constantly, 5 minutes or until thickened and bubbly; remove from heat.

Stir in shrimp mixture, rice, lemon juice, and ⅛ teaspoon pepper. Spoon 1 cup shrimp mixture into each of four individual ovenproof serving dishes coated with cooking spray.

Combine breadcrumbs, cheese, and parsley; sprinkle 2 tablespoons over each serving. Place dishes on a baking sheet. Bake at 350° for 15 minutes or until thoroughly heated. Yield: 4 servings.

PER SERVING: 297 CALORIES (25% FROM FAT)
FAT 8.4G (SATURATED FAT 0.8G)
PROTEIN 27.9G CARBOHYDRATE 27.2G
CHOLESTEROL 165MG SODIUM 350MG

CREAMY FOUR-CHEESE MACARONI

The combination of these cheeses packs all the flavor. Fresh Parmesan and good extra-sharp Cheddar are musts.

⅓ cup all-purpose flour
2⅔ cups 1% low-fat milk
¾ cup (3 ounces) shredded fontina cheese or Swiss cheese
½ cup freshly grated Parmesan cheese
½ cup (2 ounces) shredded extra-sharp Cheddar cheese
3 ounces light loaf process cheese spread
6 cups cooked elbow macaroni (cooked without salt or fat)
¼ teaspoon salt
Vegetable cooking spray
⅓ cup crushed onion Melba toast (about 12 pieces)
1 tablespoon reduced-calorie margarine, softened

Place flour in a large saucepan. Gradually add milk, stirring with a whisk until blended. Cook over medium heat, stirring constantly, 8 minutes or until thickened. Add cheeses; cook 3 minutes or until cheeses melt, stirring often. Remove from heat; stir in pasta and salt.

Spoon mixture into a 2-quart casserole coated with cooking spray. Combine crushed toast and margarine in a small bowl; stir until well blended. Sprinkle over pasta mixture. Bake at 375° for 30 minutes or until bubbly. Yield: 8 (1-cup) servings.

PER SERVING: 350 CALORIES (29% FROM FAT)
FAT 11.2G (SATURATED FAT 6.3G)
PROTEIN 18.0G CARBOHYDRATE 42.4G
CHOLESTEROL 32MG SODIUM 497MG

Creamy Four-Cheese Macaroni

NO-BAKE ZITI

2½ cups ziti (short tubular pasta), uncooked
2 cups low-fat, low-sodium spaghetti sauce
¼ cup chopped fresh parsley
1 cup light ricotta cheese
¼ teaspoon pepper
⅛ teaspoon salt
½ cup (2 ounces) shredded part-skim mozzarella cheese

Cook pasta according to package directions, omitting salt and fat. Drain pasta, and set aside.

Combine spaghetti sauce and parsley in a medium saucepan; place over medium heat, and cook 12 minutes, stirring occasionally. Remove from heat. Combine pasta, ricotta cheese, pepper, and salt in a large bowl; toss well.

Spoon pasta mixture evenly onto individual serving plates; top evenly with spaghetti sauce mixture and mozzarella cheese. Yield: 4 servings.

PER SERVING: 338 CALORIES (17% FROM FAT)
FAT 6.2G (SATURATED FAT 3.1G)
PROTEIN 18.8G CARBOHYDRATE 53.0G
CHOLESTEROL 21MG SODIUM 556MG

Spinach and Cheese Manicotti

8 manicotti shells, uncooked
1 (10-ounce) package frozen chopped spinach
Olive oil-flavored vegetable cooking spray
2 teaspoons olive oil
⅔ cup finely chopped onion
2 cloves garlic, minced
½ cup freshly grated Parmesan cheese, divided
1 (15-ounce) carton light ricotta cheese
2 egg whites, lightly beaten
¼ teaspoon dried crushed red pepper
⅛ teaspoon ground nutmeg
2 cups fat-free spaghetti sauce

Cook manicotti shells according to package directions, omitting salt and fat; drain well, and set aside.

Cook spinach according to package directions, omitting salt. Drain spinach, and press gently between paper towels to remove excess moisture.

Coat a medium saucepan with cooking spray; add oil. Place over medium-high heat until hot. Add onion and garlic; sauté 8 minutes. Transfer onion mixture to a bowl. Add spinach, ¼ cup Parmesan cheese, ricotta cheese, and next 3 ingredients; stir well. Stuff spinach mixture evenly into cooked shells.

Spread ½ cup spaghetti sauce in a 13- x 9- x 2-inch baking dish. Place filled shells over sauce. Pour remaining spaghetti sauce over shells.

Cover and bake at 375° for 30 minutes or until thoroughly heated. Sprinkle with remaining ¼ cup Parmesan cheese. Yield: 4 servings.

PER SERVING: 369 CALORIES (25% FROM FAT)
FAT 10.3G (SATURATED FAT 4.8G)
PROTEIN 25.7G   CARBOHYDRATE 47.9G
CHOLESTEROL 23MG   SODIUM 705MG

Garden Vegetable Lasagna

Vegetable cooking spray
1 teaspoon olive oil
2 cups thinly sliced fresh mushrooms
½ cup chopped onion
2 cloves garlic, minced
1 (10-ounce) package frozen chopped spinach, thawed
¾ cup finely shredded carrot
1 cup light ricotta cheese
¼ cup grated Parmesan cheese
2 egg whites, lightly beaten
1 (25½-ounce) jar fat-free spaghetti sauce
9 cooked lasagna noodles (cooked without salt or fat)
1½ cups (6 ounces) shredded part-skim mozzarella cheese

Coat a nonstick skillet with cooking spray, and add oil. Place over medium-high heat until hot. Add mushrooms, onion, and garlic; sauté until vegetables are tender and liquid evaporates.

Drain spinach, and press gently between paper towels to remove excess moisture. Add spinach and carrot to mushroom mixture; stir well.

Combine ricotta cheese, Parmesan cheese, and egg whites in a small bowl, stirring well.

Spread ⅔ cup spaghetti sauce in a 13- x 9- x 2-inch baking dish coated with cooking spray. Place 3 lasagna noodles over sauce; spoon half of ricotta cheese mixture over noodles. Top with half of vegetable mixture; spoon ⅔ cup spaghetti sauce over vegetable mixture.

Repeat layers with 3 noodles, remaining cheese mixture, remaining vegetable mixture, and ⅔ cup spaghetti sauce. Top with remaining 3 lasagna noodles and remaining spaghetti sauce. Cover and bake at 350° for 40 minutes. Uncover and sprinkle with mozzarella cheese. Bake, uncovered, 5 additional minutes or until cheese melts. Let stand 15 minutes before serving. Yield: 8 servings.

PER SERVING: 231 CALORIES (25% FROM FAT)
FAT 6.4G (SATURATED FAT 3.4G)
PROTEIN 15.5G   CARBOHYDRATE 29.7G
CHOLESTEROL 19MG   SODIUM 498MG

Spiced Pumpkin Bread with Pineapple Spread (recipe on page 82)

BASIC BREADS

*Y*ou can find breads of all shapes and flavors on the supermarket shelves. Simple to prepare and generally low in fat, these breads can be served straight from the package or dressed up as in the recipe on page 87 for Herbed Garlic Bread. However, as tasty as it is, the aroma and flavor of commercial bread can't compete with that of homemade bread fresh from the oven.

Invite your family to breakfast with Old-Fashioned Buttermilk Biscuits (page 76) or Oatmeal-Raisin Muffins (page 78). When you have a little more time, turn to pages 81 or 82 to prepare Fresh Apple Coffee Cake or a loaf of quick bread.

For evening meals, bake one of the breads made with cornmeal (page 75) or Golden Honey Rolls (page 85) that calls for yeast. If kneading is not your thing, be sure to try the No-Knead Bread on the same page to get the flavor of yeast bread without all the work.

Chile-Cheese Cornbread

CHILE-CHEESE CORNBREAD

1 cup all-purpose flour
1 tablespoon plus 1 teaspoon baking powder
¼ teaspoon salt
1 cup yellow cornmeal
¼ cup nonfat dry milk powder
1 tablespoon sugar
1 cup water
½ cup fat-free egg substitute
2 tablespoons vegetable oil
¾ cup (3 ounces) shredded reduced-fat
   Cheddar cheese
1 (4.5-ounce) can chopped green chiles, drained
Vegetable cooking spray

Combine first 6 ingredients in a medium bowl; make a well in center of mixture.

Combine water, egg substitute, and oil; add to flour mixture, stirring just until dry ingredients are moistened. Stir in cheese and chiles.

Pour batter into an 8-inch square baking dish coated with cooking spray. Bake at 375° for 30 minutes or until golden. Cut into squares. Yield: 16 squares.

PER SQUARE: 108 CALORIES (25% FROM FAT)
FAT 3.0G (SATURATED FAT 0.9G)
PROTEIN 4.7G CARBOHYDRATE 15.6G
CHOLESTEROL 4MG SODIUM 98MG

TINY CORNCAKES

¼ cup plus 2 tablespoons all-purpose flour
2 tablespoons whole wheat flour
1 teaspoon baking powder
¼ teaspoon salt
¼ cup plus 2 tablespoons cornmeal
½ teaspoon sugar
1 (8¾-ounce) can no-salt-added cream-style
   corn
¼ cup plus 2 tablespoons skim milk
2 tablespoons fat-free egg substitute
Vegetable cooking spray
No-salt-added picante sauce (optional)

Combine first 6 ingredients in a large bowl, stirring well; make a well in center of mixture. Combine corn, milk, and egg substitute, stirring well; add to flour mixture, stirring just until dry ingredients are moistened.

For each corncake, pour 2 tablespoons batter onto a hot griddle or skillet coated with cooking spray. Cook corncakes until tops are covered with bubbles and edges look cooked; turn corncakes, and cook other sides. Serve with picante sauce, if desired. Yield: 15 (3-inch) corncakes.

PER CORNCAKE: 43 CALORIES (4% FROM FAT)
FAT 0.2G (SATURATED FAT 0.0G)
PROTEIN 1.4G CARBOHYDRATE 9.2G
CHOLESTEROL 0MG SODIUM 46MG

SPOONBREAD

2¼ cups skim milk, divided
⅔ cup cornmeal
2 tablespoons margarine, melted
⅛ teaspoon salt
¼ teaspoon pepper
1 (8-ounce) carton fat-free egg substitute
Vegetable cooking spray

Heat 2 cups milk over medium-high heat in a heavy saucepan to 180° or until tiny bubbles form around edge. (Do not boil.)

Place cornmeal in a bowl. Add remaining ¼ cup milk, margarine, salt, and pepper to cornmeal, stirring until well blended; add to hot milk in saucepan. Bring to a boil over medium-high heat, stirring constantly with a wire whisk; cook, stirring constantly, 2 minutes or until thickened. Remove from heat.

Beat egg substitute in a small bowl at high speed of an electric mixer 2 minutes or until slightly thickened. Add egg substitute to cornmeal mixture; stir until well blended. Pour mixture into a 1½-quart casserole coated with cooking spray. Bake at 375° for 30 minutes or until puffed and set; serve immediately. Yield: 4 (¾-cup) servings.

PER SERVING: 213 CALORIES (27% FROM FAT)
FAT 6.5G (SATURATED FAT 1.3G)
PROTEIN 12.3G CARBOHYDRATE 25.6G
CHOLESTEROL 3MG SODIUM 297MG

CHEDDAR POPOVERS

3 egg whites
½ cup skim milk
1 tablespoon reduced-calorie stick margarine, melted
⅓ cup bread flour
2 tablespoons whole wheat flour
⅛ teaspoon salt
Vegetable cooking spray
2 tablespoons shredded reduced-fat sharp Cheddar cheese

Beat egg whites at high speed of an electric mixer until foamy. Add milk and margarine to egg whites; beat at medium speed until well blended. Gradually add flours and salt, beating until mixture is smooth.

Coat muffin pan with cooking spray. Heat at 450° for 2 to 3 minutes or until hot. Remove from oven. Pour 1 tablespoon batter into each cup; sprinkle each with 1 teaspoon cheese. Fill cups three-fourths full with remaining batter.

Bake popovers at 375° for 45 minutes. Cut a small slit in top of each popover, and bake 5 additional minutes. Serve immediately. Yield: 6 popovers.

PER POPOVER: 70 CALORIES (27% FROM FAT)
FAT 2.1G (SATURATED FAT 0.5G)
PROTEIN 4.3G   CARBOHYDRATE 8.5G
CHOLESTEROL 2MG   SODIUM 120MG

SCOTTISH OAT SCONES

1¼ cups all-purpose flour
¼ cup whole wheat flour
1 tablespoon baking powder
¼ teaspoon salt
1¼ cups quick-cooking oats, uncooked
⅓ cup currants
3 tablespoons sugar
1 egg, lightly beaten
¼ cup plus 2 tablespoons skim milk
¼ cup stick margarine, melted
2 teaspoons sugar
¼ teaspoon ground cinnamon

Combine first 7 ingredients in a large bowl. Combine egg, milk, and margarine; add to flour mixture, stirring with a fork just until dry ingredients are moistened. (Dough will be stiff and sticky.)

Turn dough out onto a lightly floured surface, and knead lightly 4 or 5 times. Roll dough into an 8-inch circle. Combine 2 teaspoons sugar and cinnamon; sprinkle over dough. Cut into 16 wedges with a sharp knife.

Place wedges on an ungreased baking sheet. Bake at 375° for 10 minutes or until golden. Yield: 16 scones.

PER SCONE: 118 CALORIES (29% FROM FAT)
FAT 3.8G (SATURATED FAT 0.8G)
PROTEIN 3.0G   CARBOHYDRATE 18.6G
CHOLESTEROL 14MG   SODIUM 79MG

OLD-FASHIONED BUTTERMILK BISCUITS

1¾ cups all-purpose flour
2 teaspoons baking powder
½ teaspoon baking soda
½ teaspoon salt
½ teaspoon sugar
⅔ cup nonfat buttermilk
2 tablespoons vegetable oil
1 tablespoon nonfat sour cream
Butter-flavored vegetable cooking spray

Combine first 5 ingredients in a medium bowl; make a well in center of mixture.

Combine buttermilk, oil, and sour cream; add to dry ingredients, stirring just until moistened.

Turn dough out onto a lightly floured surface. Knead 5 or 6 times. Roll dough to ¾-inch thickness; cut into rounds with a 2½-inch biscuit cutter. Place on an ungreased baking sheet. Coat rounds lightly with cooking spray. Bake at 400° for 8 to 10 minutes or until lightly browned. Yield: 1 dozen.

PER BISCUIT: 94 CALORIES (25% FROM FAT)
FAT 2.6G (SATURATED FAT 0.4G)
PROTEIN 2.5G   CARBOHYDRATE 15.1G
CHOLESTEROL 0MG   SODIUM 166MG

Old-Fashioned Buttermilk Biscuits

MAPLE-WALNUT MUFFINS

2¼ cups all-purpose flour
1 teaspoon baking powder
½ teaspoon baking soda
¼ teaspoon salt
1 cup sugar
½ cup chilled reduced-calorie stick margarine, cut into small pieces
3 egg whites, lightly beaten
2 tablespoons maple syrup
1 teaspoon imitation maple flavoring
1 (8-ounce) carton plain nonfat yogurt
Vegetable cooking spray
¼ cup chopped walnuts

Combine first 5 ingredients in a large bowl; cut in margarine with a pastry blender or two knives until mixture resembles coarse meal.

Combine egg whites and next 3 ingredients; add to flour mixture, stirring just until dry ingredients are moistened.

Spoon batter into muffin pans coated with cooking spray; sprinkle walnuts evenly over batter. Bake at 350° for 25 minutes or until muffins spring back when touched lightly in center. Remove from pans immediately; cool on wire racks. Yield: 1½ dozen.

PER MUFFIN: 148 CALORIES (27% FROM FAT)
FAT 4.4G (SATURATED FAT 0.8G)
PROTEIN 3.0G   CARBOHYDRATE 24.9G
CHOLESTEROL 0MG   SODIUM 124MG

Muffin Magic

When making muffins, it's important to follow the recommended mixing technique. Combine dry ingredients, making a well in center. Add liquid, and stir just until dry ingredients are moistened. Overmixing causes peaks and tunnels. Do not use a mixer unless the recipe calls for it.

OATMEAL-RAISIN MUFFINS

1 cup quick-cooking oats, uncooked
1 cup nonfat buttermilk
¼ cup plus 2 tablespoons firmly packed brown sugar
¼ cup unsweetened applesauce
¼ cup fat-free egg substitute
3 tablespoons vegetable oil
1 cup all-purpose flour
1 teaspoon baking powder
¾ teaspoon baking soda
¼ teaspoon salt
⅓ cup raisins
Vegetable cooking spray

Combine oats and buttermilk in a large bowl; let stand 1 hour. Add brown sugar and next 3 ingredients to oat mixture, stirring well. Combine flour and next 3 ingredients; add to oat mixture, stirring just until moistened. Fold in raisins.

Spoon batter into muffin pans coated with cooking spray, filling three-fourths full. Bake at 400° for 15 minutes or until golden. Yield: 1 dozen.

PER MUFFIN: 148 CALORIES (26% FROM FAT)
FAT 4.3G (SATURATED FAT 0.8G)
PROTEIN 3.6G   CARBOHYDRATE 24.4G
CHOLESTEROL 1MG   SODIUM 82MG

WHOLE WHEAT-BANANA MUFFINS

1 cup all-purpose flour
1 cup whole wheat flour
1 teaspoon baking powder
1 teaspoon baking soda
½ teaspoon salt
¼ cup toasted wheat germ
1⅓ cups mashed ripe banana (about 3 large)
½ cup plus 2 tablespoons sugar
¼ cup vegetable oil
1 egg, lightly beaten
Vegetable cooking spray

Whole Wheat-Banana Muffins

Combine first 6 ingredients in a large bowl; make a well in center of mixture.

Combine banana and next 3 ingredients; add to flour mixture, stirring just until dry ingredients are moistened.

Spoon batter into muffin pans coated with cooking spray, filling two-thirds full. Bake at 350° for 20 minutes. Yield: 16 muffins.

PER MUFFIN: 148 CALORIES (27% FROM FAT)
FAT 4.4G (SATURATED FAT 0.7G)
PROTEIN 2.8G   CARBOHYDRATE 25.6G
CHOLESTEROL 14MG   SODIUM 157MG

WHOLE WHEAT-BANANA LOAF

Prepare batter as directed; spoon into a 9- x 5- x 3-inch loafpan coated with cooking spray. Bake at 400° for 40 to 45 minutes or until a wooden pick inserted in center comes out clean. Yield: 18 (½-inch) slices.

PER SLICE: 131 CALORIES (27% FROM FAT)
FAT 3.9G (SATURATED FAT 0.6G)
PROTEIN 2.5G   CARBOHYDRATE 22.8G
CHOLESTEROL 12MG   SODIUM 140MG

Fresh Apple Coffee Cake

FRESH APPLE COFFEE CAKE

This breakfast bread easily doubles as a dessert. Rome or Granny Smith apples provide the best flavor, but any cooking apple will do.

4 cups finely chopped cooking apple
½ cup unsweetened orange juice, divided
1½ teaspoons ground cinnamon
½ cup stick margarine, softened
1 cup sugar
1 (8-ounce) carton fat-free egg substitute
¼ cup skim milk
3 cups sifted cake flour
2 teaspoons baking powder
¼ teaspoon salt
2½ teaspoons vanilla extract
Vegetable cooking spray
2 tablespoons brown sugar

Combine apple, ¼ cup orange juice, and cinnamon; set aside.

Beat margarine at medium speed of an electric mixer until creamy; gradually add 1 cup sugar, beating until light and fluffy (about 5 minutes). Add egg substitute; beat at medium speed 4 minutes or until well blended.

Combine remaining ¼ cup orange juice and milk. Combine flour, baking powder, and salt; add to margarine mixture alternately with milk mixture, beginning and ending with flour mixture. Stir in vanilla.

Pour half of batter into a 10-inch tube pan coated with cooking spray; top with half of apple mixture. Pour remaining batter into pan, and top with remaining apple mixture; sprinkle with brown sugar.

Bake at 350° for 1 hour or until a wooden pick inserted in center comes out clean. Cool in pan on a wire rack 10 minutes; remove from pan, and cool completely on wire rack. Yield: 16 servings.

PER SERVING: 203 CALORIES (27% FROM FAT)
FAT 6.0G (SATURATED FAT 1.2G)
PROTEIN 3.2G CARBOHYDRATE 34.4G
CHOLESTEROL 0MG SODIUM 128MG

STICKY LEMON BREAD

Pierce this bread with a meat fork to allow the lemon syrup to soak in thoroughly.

¼ cup plus 2 tablespoons stick margarine, softened
⅔ cup sugar
¼ cup fat-free egg substitute
1 teaspoon grated lemon rind
½ teaspoon vanilla extract
2¼ cups all-purpose flour
¾ teaspoon baking powder
½ teaspoon baking soda
¼ teaspoon salt
1 (8-ounce) carton lemon low-fat yogurt
Baking spray with flour
½ cup sugar
½ cup fresh lemon juice

Beat margarine at medium speed of an electric mixer until creamy; gradually add ⅔ cup sugar, beating at medium speed until light and fluffy (about 5 minutes). Add egg substitute, lemon rind, and vanilla; beat until well blended.

Combine flour and next 3 ingredients. Add flour mixture to margarine mixture alternately with yogurt, beginning and ending with flour mixture. Beat at low speed after each addition until blended.

Pour batter into an 8½- x 4½- x 3-inch loafpan coated with baking spray. Bake at 350° for 55 minutes or until a wooden pick inserted in center comes out clean. Remove from oven; cool in pan on a wire rack.

Combine ½ cup sugar and lemon juice in a saucepan; bring to a boil, and boil 1 minute. Remove from heat.

Pierce top of bread several times with a meat fork. Pour lemon juice mixture over bread; cool in pan 10 minutes. Remove from pan; cool completely on a wire rack. Yield: 16 (½-inch) slices.

PER SLICE: 177 CALORIES (23% FROM FAT)
FAT 4.6G (SATURATED FAT 0.9G)
PROTEIN 2.6G CARBOHYDRATE 31.9G
CHOLESTEROL 0MG SODIUM 142MG

Spiced Pumpkin Bread with Pineapple Spread

(pictured on page 72)

2 cups sifted cake flour
2 teaspoons baking powder
¼ teaspoon baking soda
¼ teaspoon salt
⅔ cup firmly packed brown sugar
1 teaspoon ground cinnamon
¼ teaspoon ground ginger
¼ teaspoon ground cloves
2 eggs, lightly beaten
1 cup canned pumpkin
¼ cup unsweetened applesauce
3 tablespoons vegetable oil
1 teaspoon vanilla extract
Vegetable cooking spray
Pineapple Spread

Combine first 8 ingredients in a medium bowl; make a well in center of mixture. Combine eggs and next 4 ingredients; add to flour mixture, stirring just until dry ingredients are moistened.

Spoon batter into a 9- x 5- x 3-inch loafpan coated with cooking spray. Bake at 350° for 45 to 50 minutes or until a wooden pick inserted in center comes out clean. Cool in pan 10 minutes; remove from pan, and cool completely on a wire rack. Cut into ½-inch slices. Top each slice with about 1 tablespoon Pineapple Spread. Yield: 18 servings.

Pineapple Spread

1 (8-ounce) tub-style light cream cheese, softened
1 (8-ounce) can crushed pineapple in juice, drained
1½ tablespoons honey
⅛ teaspoon ground ginger

Combine all ingredients; stir well. Cover and chill at least 30 minutes. Yield: 1⅓ cups.

Per Serving: 150 Calories (31% from Fat)
Fat 5.2g (Saturated Fat 1.9g)
Protein 3.2g Carbohydrate 23.0g
Cholesterol 32mg Sodium 133mg

Strawberry Bread

Fresh strawberries keep this bread so moist that it needs very little oil.

2 cups sifted cake flour
1 teaspoon baking soda
¼ teaspoon salt
¾ cup sugar
1 teaspoon ground cinnamon
2 eggs, lightly beaten
¼ cup skim milk
2 tablespoons vegetable oil
1 cup chopped fresh strawberries
1 tablespoon cake flour
Vegetable cooking spray

Combine first 5 ingredients in a medium bowl; make a well in center of mixture.

Combine eggs, milk, and oil; add to flour mixture, stirring just until dry ingredients are moistened.

Dredge strawberries in 1 tablespoon flour; gently fold into batter.

Spoon batter into an 8½- x 4½- x 3-inch loafpan coated with cooking spray. Bake at 350° for 50 to 55 minutes. Cool in pan 5 minutes; remove from pan, and cool completely on a wire rack. Yield: 16 (½-inch) slices.

Per Slice: 117 Calories (19% from Fat)
Fat 2.5g (Saturated Fat 0.5g)
Protein 2.2g Carbohydrate 21.4g
Cholesterol 28mg Sodium 126mg

Strawberry Bread

Golden Honey Rolls

Cut dough into 2-inch rounds with a biscuit cutter.

Fold each round of dough in half, and place in a baking pan.

GOLDEN HONEY ROLLS

½ cup water
¼ cup stick margarine
¼ cup honey
1½ cups whole wheat flour, divided
2 packages rapid-rise yeast
¾ teaspoon salt
½ cup nonfat sour cream
½ cup fat-free egg substitute
2¼ to 2½ cups all-purpose flour
Butter-flavored vegetable cooking spray

Combine first 3 ingredients in a small saucepan; cook over low heat until margarine melts, stirring occasionally. Cool to 125° to 130°.

Sift together 1 cup whole wheat flour, yeast, and salt into a large bowl. Gradually add honey mixture to flour mixture, beating at low speed of an electric mixer after each addition. Add sour cream and egg substitute, beating just until blended. Stir in remaining ½ cup whole wheat flour and enough all-purpose flour to make a soft dough.

Turn out dough onto a lightly floured surface; knead until smooth and elastic (6 to 8 minutes). Cover and let rest 10 minutes. Pat or roll dough to ½-inch thickness; cut with a 2-inch biscuit cutter to make 28 rounds. Fold each round in half; place in a 13- x 9- x 2-inch pan coated with cooking spray. Coat dough with cooking spray.

Cover and let rise in a warm place (85°), free from drafts, 35 minutes or until doubled in bulk. Bake at 400° for 13 to 15 minutes or until lightly browned. Yield: 28 rolls.

PER ROLL: 91 CALORIES (21% FROM FAT)
FAT 2.1G (SATURATED FAT 0.4G)
PROTEIN 2.9G CARBOHYDRATE 15.4G
CHOLESTEROL 0MG SODIUM 92MG

NO-KNEAD BREAD

You'll be surprised at how easy this bread is to make. Just combine the ingredients in a large airtight plastic container, and seal the lid. The dough "burps" the lid off the container when it has finished rising. In our Test Kitchens, we used a Tupperware® container for best results.

3 packages active dry yeast
3¾ cups warm water (105° to 115°)
10 cups all-purpose flour
¼ cup plus 2 tablespoons sugar
¼ cup plus 2 tablespoons stick margarine, melted
1 tablespoon salt
2 eggs, lightly beaten
Vegetable cooking spray

Combine yeast and warm water in a 7-quart airtight plastic container, stirring mixture well; let stand 5 minutes. Add flour and next 4 ingredients, stirring until well blended. Cover with lid, and seal. Let stand at room temperature 1 hour or until lid pops off.

Spoon dough evenly into three 9- x 5- x 3-inch loafpans coated with cooking spray. Cover and let rise in a warm place (85°), free from drafts, 30 minutes or until doubled in bulk. Bake at 350° for 40 minutes or until loaves sound hollow when tapped. Yield: 3 loaves, 16 slices each.

PER SLICE: 110 CALORIES (16% FROM FAT)
FAT 1.9G (SATURATED FAT 0.4G)
PROTEIN 2.9G CARBOHYDRATE 20.1G
CHOLESTEROL 9MG SODIUM 166MG

Herbed Garlic Bread

HERBED GARLIC BREAD

¼ cup reduced-calorie stick margarine,
   softened
1½ tablespoons freshly grated Parmesan
   cheese
2 teaspoons minced fresh parsley
2 teaspoons minced fresh basil
¼ teaspoon garlic powder
12 (¾-inch-thick) slices French bread

Combine first 5 ingredients; stir well. Spread evenly on 1 side of bread slices. Wrap bread in aluminum foil, and bake at 400° for 15 minutes. Yield: 12 (¾-inch) slices.

PER SLICE: 103 CALORIES (26% FROM FAT)
FAT 3.0G (SATURATED FAT 0.5G)
PROTEIN 2.6G CARBOHYDRATE 15.8G
CHOLESTEROL 1MG SODIUM 203MG

MONKEY BREAD

2 (1-pound) loaves frozen white bread
   dough
1 cup sugar
¼ cup firmly packed brown sugar
¼ cup 1% low-fat milk
1 tablespoon reduced-calorie stick margarine
1¼ teaspoons ground cinnamon
¼ cup sugar
½ teaspoon ground cinnamon
Vegetable cooking spray

Thaw bread dough in refrigerator 12 hours.

Combine 1 cup sugar and next 4 ingredients in a small saucepan; bring to a boil. Cook, stirring constantly, 1 minute. Remove sugar syrup from heat; cool 10 minutes.

Cut each loaf of dough into 24 equal portions. Combine ¼ cup sugar and ½ teaspoon cinnamon in a shallow dish; stir well. Roll each portion of dough in sugar mixture, and layer dough in a 12-cup Bundt pan coated with cooking spray. Pour sugar syrup over dough; cover and let rise in a warm place (85°), free from drafts, 35 minutes or until doubled in bulk.

Bake at 350° for 25 minutes or until lightly browned. Immediately loosen edges of bread with a knife. Place a serving plate, upside down, over pan; invert bread onto plate. Remove pan, and drizzle any remaining syrup over bread. Yield: 24 servings.

PER SERVING: 201 CALORIES (10% FROM FAT)
FAT 2.2G (SATURATED FAT 0.5G)
PROTEIN 5.2G CARBOHYDRATE 40.1G
CHOLESTEROL 0MG SODIUM 302MG

CINNAMON-RAISIN BATTER BREAD

1½ cups all-purpose flour
2 tablespoons sugar
1 teaspoon ground cinnamon
¼ teaspoon salt
¼ teaspoon ground allspice
1 package active dry yeast
1 cup skim milk
¼ cup molasses
2 tablespoons stick margarine
1 egg
1½ cups all-purpose flour
½ cup raisins
Vegetable cooking spray

Combine first 6 ingredients in a large bowl; stir well. Combine milk, molasses, and margarine in a small saucepan; cook over medium heat until very warm (120° to 130°). Gradually add to flour mixture, beating at low speed of an electric mixer until smooth. Add egg; beat at low speed until blended. Beat batter 3 additional minutes at medium speed. Stir in 1½ cups flour and raisins.

Spoon batter into a 9- x 5- x 3-inch loafpan coated with cooking spray. Cover and let rise in a warm place (85°), free from drafts, 40 minutes or until doubled in bulk. Bake at 350° for 35 to 40 minutes or until golden. Remove from pan, and cool on a wire rack. Yield: 18 (½-inch) slices.

PER SLICE: 126 CALORIES (13% FROM FAT)
FAT 1.8G (SATURATED FAT 0.4G)
PROTEIN 3.1G CARBOHYDRATE 24.4G
CHOLESTEROL 12MG SODIUM 60MG

French-Style Green Beans (recipe on page 94)

SALADS & SIDE DISHES

*S*alads and side dishes are some of the most nutritious fare around. They are most often made with fruits or vegetables and provide an abundance of vitamins, minerals, and fiber. When you keep additional ingredients and cooking methods in check, salads and side dishes can also be low in fat and calories.

But is it really possible to create low-fat versions of popular side dishes such as Creamy Pasta Salad, Green Bean Casserole, Hash Brown Casserole, and Sweet Potato Casserole? Indeed! And the following pages show you how it's done. Salads begin on page 91, and side dishes start on page 94. Turn to page 99 to discover how you can lighten other favorite side-dish recipes.

Apple Salad with Honey-Yogurt Dressing

APPLE SALAD WITH HONEY-YOGURT DRESSING

Spoon this crunchy, slightly sweet salad onto radicchio leaves for a unique presentation.

1½ cups coarsely chopped Granny Smith apple
1½ cups coarsely chopped Golden Delicious apple
1 cup thinly sliced celery
¾ cup coarsely chopped Red Delicious apple
½ cup seedless red grapes, halved
½ cup golden raisins
¼ cup coarsely chopped pecans
½ cup plain nonfat yogurt
2 tablespoons honey
1 tablespoon white wine vinegar
1½ teaspoons Dijon mustard
Radicchio leaves (optional)

Combine first 7 ingredients in a large bowl; toss mixture well.

Combine yogurt and next 3 ingredients in a bowl, stirring well with a wire whisk; add to apple mixture, tossing gently. Cover and chill 30 minutes.

Line six individual salad plates evenly with radicchio leaves, if desired. Place apple salad evenly over radicchio. Yield: 6 (1-cup) servings.

PER SERVING: 160 CALORIES (21% FROM FAT)
FAT 3.8G (SATURATED FAT 0.4G)
PROTEIN 2.2G CARBOHYDRATE 32.7G
CHOLESTEROL 0MG SODIUM 72MG

YOGURT-TOPPED FRUIT SALAD

1½ cups sliced fresh strawberries
2 small bananas, peeled and sliced
1 medium-size orange, peeled and sectioned
6 green leaf lettuce leaves
¼ cup vanilla low-fat yogurt
1 tablespoon creamy peanut butter
1 tablespoon chopped roasted, salted peanuts

Combine first 3 ingredients in a bowl, and toss gently. Spoon evenly onto individual lettuce-lined salad plates.

Combine yogurt and peanut butter, stirring well. Spoon over fruit. Sprinkle with peanuts; serve immediately. Yield: 6 servings.

PER SERVING: 89 CALORIES (30% FROM FAT)
FAT 3.0G (SATURATED FAT 0.6G)
PROTEIN 2.6G CARBOHYDRATE 14.8G
CHOLESTEROL 0MG SODIUM 40MG

MANDARIN-ROMAINE SALAD

6 cups torn romaine lettuce
½ cup diced purple onion
1 (11-ounce) can mandarin oranges in light syrup, drained
¼ cup unsweetened orange juice
1 teaspoon sugar
1 teaspoon peeled, grated gingerroot
1 teaspoon low-sodium soy sauce
1 teaspoon dark sesame oil

Combine first 3 ingredients in a large bowl, tossing gently.

Combine orange juice and remaining 4 ingredients. Pour over lettuce mixture, and toss gently. Serve immediately. Yield: 6 (1-cup) servings.

PER SERVING: 44 CALORIES (16% FROM FAT)
FAT 0.8G (SATURATED FAT 0.1G)
PROTEIN 0.7G CARBOHYDRATE 8.6G
CHOLESTEROL 0MG SODIUM 26MG

Apricot-Pineapple Congealed Salad

APRICOT-PINEAPPLE CONGEALED SALADS

1 (8-ounce) can unsweetened crushed
   pineapple, undrained
1 (16-ounce) can apricot halves in juice,
   undrained
1 (12-ounce) can apricot nectar
2 envelopes unflavored gelatin
Vegetable cooking spray
Lettuce leaves (optional)
¼ cup plus 2 tablespoons pineapple low-fat
   yogurt

Drain crushed pineapple, reserving liquid. Drain apricot halves, reserving 2 tablespoons liquid. Set aside 12 apricot halves, and reserve remaining apricot halves for another use.

Combine apricot nectar and reserved pineapple and apricot liquids in a saucepan. Sprinkle gelatin over mixture; let stand 1 minute. Cook mixture over low heat, stirring until gelatin dissolves, about 2 minutes.

Pour mixture into a bowl; cover and chill 1 hour or until consistency of unbeaten egg white. Fold in crushed pineapple.

Thinly slice 6 apricot halves, and arrange in six ½-cup molds coated with cooking spray; top each with ⅓ cup gelatin mixture. Cover molds, and chill until firm.

Cut remaining 6 apricot halves in half, and set aside. Unmold gelatin mixture onto individual lettuce-lined salad plates. Top each salad with 1 tablespoon yogurt, and serve each with 2 apricot slices. Yield: 6 servings.

PER SERVING: 110 CALORIES (4% FROM FAT)
FAT 0.5G (SATURATED FAT 0.2G)
PROTEIN 3.6G   CARBOHYDRATE 24.4G
CHOLESTEROL 1MG   SODIUM 18MG

WHITE CORN SALAD

2 cups frozen shoepeg white corn, thawed
¾ cup chopped tomato
½ cup chopped cucumber
2 tablespoons chopped green pepper
3 tablespoons white wine vinegar
1½ teaspoons olive oil
1 teaspoon Dijon mustard
¼ teaspoon salt
⅛ teaspoon pepper
1 clove garlic, minced

Combine first 4 ingredients in a large bowl; toss. Combine vinegar and remaining 5 ingredients in a jar. Cover tightly; shake vigorously. Pour over corn mixture; toss well. Yield: 4 (¾-cup) servings.

PER SERVING: 96 CALORIES (19% FROM FAT)
FAT 2.0G (SATURATED FAT 0.3G)
PROTEIN 2.9G CARBOHYDRATE 19.4G
CHOLESTEROL 0MG SODIUM 192MG

CREAMY PASTA SALAD

4½ ounces rotini (corkscrew pasta), uncooked
16 cherry tomatoes, quartered
2 tablespoons sliced ripe olives
½ cup nonfat sour cream
¼ cup reduced-calorie mayonnaise
1 tablespoon prepared mustard
2 teaspoons sugar
2 teaspoons white wine vinegar
½ teaspoon salt
¼ teaspoon pepper
⅛ teaspoon garlic powder

Cook pasta according to package directions, omitting salt and fat. Drain. Rinse under cold water; drain. Combine pasta, tomatoes, and olives in a bowl.
Combine sour cream and remaining 7 ingredients in a small bowl; stir well. Add pasta mixture; toss to combine. Yield: 5 (1-cup) servings.

PER SERVING: 169 CALORIES (25% FROM FAT)
FAT 4.6G (SATURATED FAT 0.7G)
PROTEIN 5.6G CARBOHYDRATE 25.9G
CHOLESTEROL 4MG SODIUM 439MG

RANCH SLAW

¼ cup sliced green onions
1 (10-ounce) bag angel hair slaw
⅓ cup commercial fat-free Ranch-style dressing
1 (11-ounce) can mandarin oranges in light syrup, well drained
½ ripe avocado, peeled, pitted, and chopped

Combine green onions and slaw in a large bowl. Add dressing, and toss to coat. Add oranges and avocado; toss gently. Serve immediately. Yield: 6 (¾-cup) servings.
Note: This recipe may be easily doubled.

PER SERVING: 80 CALORIES (24% FROM FAT)
FAT 2.1G (SATURATED FAT 0.3G)
PROTEIN 1.3G CARBOHYDRATE 14.7G
CHOLESTEROL 0MG SODIUM 150MG

EASY REFRIGERATOR PICKLES

6 cups thinly sliced cucumber (about 2 pounds)
2 cups thinly sliced onion
1½ cups white vinegar
1 cup sugar
½ teaspoon salt
½ teaspoon mustard seeds
½ teaspoon celery seeds
½ teaspoon ground turmeric

Place half of cucumber slices in a large glass bowl; top with half of onion slices. Repeat layers.
Combine vinegar and remaining 5 ingredients in a saucepan; stir well. Bring to a boil; boil 1 minute.
Pour vinegar mixture over cucumber and onion; cool. Cover and marinate in refrigerator 4 days. Store in refrigerator up to 1 month. Yield: 26 (¼-cup) servings.

PER SERVING: 40 CALORIES (2% FROM FAT)
FAT 0.1G (SATURATED FAT 0.0G)
PROTEIN 0.4G CARBOHYDRATE 10.3G
CHOLESTEROL 0MG SODIUM 46MG

Stovetop "Baked" Beans

1 tablespoon margarine
1¼ cups chopped onion
¾ cup chopped green pepper
2 cloves garlic, minced
1 cup reduced-calorie ketchup
¼ cup firmly packed brown sugar
¼ cup maple syrup
2 tablespoons Worcestershire sauce
2 teaspoons barbecue liquid smoke (such as Hickory Liquid Smoke)
2 teaspoons prepared mustard
1 (16-ounce) can red beans, drained
1 (15.8-ounce) can Great Northern beans, drained

Melt margarine in a saucepan over medium-high heat. Add onion, pepper, and garlic; sauté 4 minutes. Stir in ketchup and remaining ingredients; bring to a boil. Reduce heat; simmer 15 minutes, stirring occasionally. Yield: 8 (½-cup) servings.

PER SERVING: 179 CALORIES (10% FROM FAT)
FAT 1.9G (SATURATED FAT 0.4G)
PROTEIN 6.0G CARBOHYDRATE 34.6G
CHOLESTEROL 0MG SODIUM 331MG

French-Style Green Beans

(pictured on page 88)

¾ pound fresh green beans
1 tablespoon nonfat margarine
¾ cup canned low-sodium chicken broth
¼ teaspoon freshly ground pepper
⅛ teaspoon salt
1½ teaspoons cornstarch
1 tablespoon water
2 teaspoons lemon juice
2 tablespoons sliced almonds, toasted

Wash beans; trim ends, and remove strings. Slice beans in half lengthwise. Melt margarine in a large skillet. Add beans, and sauté 5 minutes. Add broth, pepper, and salt. Bring to a boil. Cover, reduce heat, and simmer 15 minutes.

Combine cornstarch and water; pour over bean mixture. Cook, stirring constantly, 1 minute. Stir in lemon juice. Just before serving, sprinkle with almonds. Yield: 4 (½-cup) servings.

PER SERVING: 49 CALORIES (24% FROM FAT)
FAT 1.3G (SATURATED FAT 0.2G)
PROTEIN 2.4G CARBOHYDRATE 8.1G
CHOLESTEROL 0MG SODIUM 113MG

Green Bean Casserole

Vegetable cooking spray
¼ cup finely chopped onion
2 tablespoons all-purpose flour
1 cup skim milk
½ cup (2 ounces) shredded reduced-sodium, reduced-fat Swiss cheese
½ cup low-fat sour cream
1 teaspoon sugar
½ teaspoon salt
2 (9-ounce) packages frozen French-style green beans, thawed and drained
1 egg white, lightly beaten
1½ cups herb-seasoned stuffing mix
2 teaspoons margarine, melted

Coat a medium saucepan with cooking spray; place over medium heat until hot. Add onion; sauté 5 minutes or until onion is tender. Add flour, and cook, stirring constantly, 1 minute. Gradually add milk, stirring until blended. Stir in cheese and next 3 ingredients; cook, stirring constantly, 5 minutes or until thickened and bubbly.

Place green beans in an 8-inch square baking dish; pour Swiss cheese sauce over beans. Combine egg white, stuffing mix, and margarine in a bowl; stir well, and sprinkle over green bean mixture. Bake, uncovered, at 350° for 25 minutes or until thoroughly heated. Yield: 8 (½-cup) servings.

PER SERVING: 139 CALORIES (30% FROM FAT)
FAT 4.7G (SATURATED FAT 2.1G)
PROTEIN 6.9G CARBOHYDRATE 18.7G
CHOLESTEROL 11MG SODIUM 382MG

Green Bean Casserole

SOUTHERN-STYLE BLACK-EYED PEAS

4 cups shelled fresh black-eyed peas
2 cups water
¾ cup minced onion
½ cup chopped lean cooked ham
½ teaspoon salt
¼ teaspoon pepper

Combine all ingredients in a large saucepan. Bring to a boil; cover, reduce heat, and simmer 30 minutes or until peas are tender, stirring occasionally. Yield: 10 (½-cup) servings.

PER SERVING: 88 CALORIES (9% FROM FAT)
FAT 0.9G (SATURATED FAT 0.3G)
PROTEIN 6.7G CARBOHYDRATE 13.7G
CHOLESTEROL 4MG SODIUM 231MG

ORANGE-GLAZED CARROTS

1 pound carrots, scraped and cut into
    ¼-inch-thick slices
¾ cup canned no-salt-added chicken broth,
    undiluted
2 tablespoons frozen orange juice concentrate,
    thawed and undiluted
2 teaspoons sugar
¼ teaspoon ground ginger

Combine carrot and broth in a medium saucepan; bring to a boil. Cover, reduce heat, and simmer 10 minutes. Uncover carrot mixture, and cook over high heat 5 minutes.

Add orange juice concentrate, sugar, and ginger to carrot mixture, stirring well. Cook mixture over medium heat 2 to 3 additional minutes or until carrot is tender. Yield: 4 (½-cup) servings.

PER SERVING: 69 CALORIES (3% FROM FAT)
FAT 0.2G (SATURATED FAT 0.0G)
PROTEIN 1.3G CARBOHYDRATE 16.0G
CHOLESTEROL 0MG SODIUM 36MG

CAULIFLOWER WITH CHEESE SAUCE

1 medium cauliflower, broken into flowerets
1 tablespoon all-purpose flour
¾ cup skim milk, divided
⅛ teaspoon salt
⅛ teaspoon dry mustard
½ cup (2 ounces) shredded reduced-fat sharp
    Cheddar cheese
2 tablespoons nonfat sour cream
2 tablespoons (½ ounce) shredded reduced-fat
    sharp Cheddar cheese

Cook cauliflower, covered, in a small amount of boiling water 8 to 10 minutes or until tender; drain. Place cauliflower in a serving dish; set aside, and keep warm.

Combine flour and ¼ cup milk, and stir until smooth. Combine flour mixture, remaining ½ cup milk, salt, and mustard in a small saucepan; stir well. Cook over medium heat, stirring constantly, until thickened and bubbly.

Add ½ cup cheese; cook over low heat, stirring constantly, until cheese melts. Remove from heat, and stir in sour cream. Pour cheese sauce over cauliflower; sprinkle with 2 tablespoons cheese. Yield: 6 (1-cup) servings.

PER SERVING: 93 CALORIES (20% FROM FAT)
FAT 2.1G (SATURATED FAT 0.9G)
PROTEIN 8.6G CARBOHYDRATE 12.5G
CHOLESTEROL 7MG SODIUM 188MG

Cauliflower with Cheese Sauce

Corn and Broccoli Casserole

CORN AND BROCCOLI CASSEROLE

1½ teaspoons all-purpose flour
¼ teaspoon dry mustard
⅛ teaspoon salt
⅛ teaspoon pepper
½ cup 1% low-fat milk
½ cup chopped onion
1 teaspoon vegetable oil
4 cups coarsely chopped fresh broccoli
   flowerets
1 (10-ounce) package frozen whole-kernel
   corn, thawed
¼ cup grated Parmesan cheese
1 tablespoon fine, dry breadcrumbs

Combine first 4 ingredients in a 2-cup glass measuring cup. Gradually add milk, stirring well with a wire whisk. Microwave, uncovered, at HIGH 2 minutes, stirring after every minute; set milk mixture aside.

Combine onion and oil in an 8-inch square microwave-safe dish. Microwave, uncovered, at HIGH 1 minute. Stir in broccoli and corn. Cover with heavy-duty plastic wrap, and vent.

Microwave at HIGH 5 minutes, stirring after 2½ minutes. Add milk mixture; stir well. Cover and microwave at HIGH 2 to 3 minutes or until thoroughly heated. Stir in cheese; top with breadcrumbs. Microwave, uncovered, at HIGH 1 minute. Let casserole stand, uncovered, 5 minutes. Yield: 4 (1-cup) servings.

PER SERVING: 152 CALORIES (24% FROM FAT)
FAT 4.0G (SATURATED FAT 1.5G)
PROTEIN 8.4G CARBOHYDRATE 24.8G
CHOLESTEROL 5MG SODIUM 220MG

CREAMED CORN

4 ears fresh corn
2 cups 2% low-fat milk, divided
¾ cup coarsely chopped onion
½ teaspoon black peppercorns
¼ cup all-purpose flour
½ teaspoon salt

Cut off tops of corn kernels; scrape milk and remaining pulp from cobs, using dull side of a knife blade. Set kernels and corn pulp aside, and reserve 1 cob. (Discard remaining 3 cobs.)

Cut reserved cob in half. Combine cob halves, 1¾ cups low-fat milk, onion, and peppercorns in a medium saucepan; bring to a boil. Reduce heat, and simmer, uncovered, 5 minutes, stirring occasionally. Strain milk mixture, and discard cob halves, onion, and peppercorns.

Combine flour and remaining ¼ cup milk in a saucepan, stirring with a wire whisk until blended. Stir in warm milk mixture. Cook over low heat, stirring constantly, 3 minutes or until thickened. Add kernels, corn pulp, and salt; stir well. Cook over medium-low heat 15 minutes or until corn is tender, stirring often. Yield: 6 (½-cup) servings.

PER SERVING: 114 CALORIES (17% FROM FAT)
FAT 2.2G (SATURATED FAT 1.1G)
PROTEIN 4.8G CARBOHYDRATE 20.4G
CHOLESTEROL 7MG SODIUM 245MG

Fat Alert

Here are the basic methods to lower the fat in your own recipe favorites.

• Eliminate high-fat ingredients (such as margarine and oil) when possible.

• Replace regular ingredients with nonfat or low-fat versions. Examples include reduced-fat or nonfat sour cream, mayonnaise, and cheese.

• Use low-fat cooking methods, such as steaming, microwaving, and baking, instead of frying.

HASH BROWN CASSEROLE

Vegetable cooking spray
1½ cups chopped onion
3 tablespoons all-purpose flour
½ teaspoon dry mustard
¼ teaspoon salt
1¼ cups skim milk
½ cup canned low-sodium chicken broth, undiluted
1½ cups (6 ounces) shredded reduced-fat sharp Cheddar cheese
¾ cup (3 ounces) shredded Swiss cheese
½ teaspoon pepper
1 cup nonfat sour cream
1 (32-ounce) package frozen Southern-style hash brown potatoes, thawed
Paprika

Coat a medium saucepan with cooking spray; place over medium heat until hot. Add onion, and sauté 3 minutes or until tender. Add flour, mustard, and salt; stir well, and cook 1 additional minute. Remove from heat; gradually add milk and broth, stirring with a wire whisk until blended.

Cook over medium heat, stirring constantly, 5 minutes or until thickened. Remove from heat; add cheeses and pepper, stirring until cheeses melt. Stir in sour cream.

Combine cheese mixture and potatoes; stir well. Spoon into a 13- x 9- x 2-inch baking dish coated with cooking spray. Sprinkle with paprika. Cover and bake at 350° for 35 minutes. Uncover and bake 35 additional minutes. Yield: 8 (1-cup) servings.

PER SERVING: 247 CALORIES (27% FROM FAT)
FAT 7.4G (SATURATED FAT 4.3G)
PROTEIN 14.8G CARBOHYDRATE 29.5G
CHOLESTEROL 25MG SODIUM 309MG

Scalloped Potatoes with Cheese

SCALLOPED POTATOES WITH CHEESE

1 clove garlic, halved
Butter-flavored vegetable cooking spray
3 pounds medium-size red potatoes, peeled and
      cut into ⅛-inch slices
2 tablespoons margarine, melted
½ teaspoon salt
¼ teaspoon pepper
½ cup (2 ounces) shredded Cheddar cheese
1 cup skim milk

Rub a 10- x 6- x 2-inch baking dish with cut sides
of garlic halves; discard garlic. Coat dish with cooking spray. Arrange half of potato slices in dish, and
drizzle with half of margarine. Sprinkle half of salt
and pepper over potato, and top with half of
cheese. Repeat layers.

Bring milk to a boil in a small saucepan over low
heat; pour hot milk over potato mixture. Bake,
uncovered, at 425° for 40 minutes or until potato is
tender. Yield: 7 (1-cup) servings.

PER SERVING: 228 CALORIES (25% FROM FAT)
FAT 6.3G (SATURATED FAT 2.4G)
PROTEIN 7.2G CARBOHYDRATE 36.8G
CHOLESTEROL 9MG SODIUM 285MG

SWEET POTATO CASSEROLE

2 egg whites, lightly beaten
3 cups cooked, mashed sweet potato
⅓ cup firmly packed brown sugar
⅓ cup skim milk
2 tablespoons reduced-calorie margarine, melted
1 teaspoon vanilla extract
½ teaspoon salt
Vegetable cooking spray
½ cup firmly packed brown sugar
¼ cup all-purpose flour
2 tablespoons chilled reduced-calorie stick
      margarine
⅓ cup chopped pecans

Combine first 7 ingredients; stir well. Spoon mixture into an 8-inch square baking dish coated with
cooking spray.

Combine ½ cup brown sugar and flour in a bowl;
cut in chilled margarine with a pastry blender or
two knives until mixture is crumbly. Stir in pecans;
sprinkle over sweet potato mixture. Bake at 350°
for 30 minutes. Yield: 8 (½-cup) servings.

PER SERVING: 273 CALORIES (24% FROM FAT)
FAT 7.4G (SATURATED FAT 0.9G)
PROTEIN 3.5G CARBOHYDRATE 49.8G
CHOLESTEROL 0MG SODIUM 242MG

SUMMER SQUASH BAKE

2 pounds yellow squash, cut into ¼-inch-thick
      slices
½ cup chopped onion
½ cup shredded carrot
½ cup (2 ounces) shredded reduced-fat
      Cheddar cheese
½ cup egg substitute with cheese
1 teaspoon low-sodium Worcestershire sauce
¼ teaspoon salt
¼ teaspoon pepper
1 (4-ounce) jar diced pimiento, drained
Vegetable cooking spray
3 tablespoons fine, dry breadcrumbs
1 tablespoon chopped fresh parsley
2 teaspoons chopped fresh oregano
¼ teaspoon paprika

Place first 3 ingredients in a steamer basket over
boiling water; cover and steam 12 to 15 minutes or
until vegetables are tender.

Combine steamed vegetables, cheese, and next 5
ingredients; stir well. Spoon mixture into a shallow
2-quart casserole coated with cooking spray.

Combine breadcrumbs and remaining 3 ingredients; stir well. Sprinkle over squash mixture. Bake,
uncovered, at 350° for 25 to 30 minutes or until
thoroughly heated. Yield: 10 servings.

PER SERVING: 62 CALORIES (30% FROM FAT)
FAT 2.1G (SATURATED FAT 0.8G)
PROTEIN 4.6G CARBOHYDRATE 7.1G
CHOLESTEROL 4MG SODIUM 164MG

FRUIT-GLAZED ACORN SQUASH

Acorn squash are very firm, so microwave them for a few minutes before slicing.
This also shortens the baking time for this recipe.

2 small acorn squash (about 2 pounds)
¾ cup unsweetened pineapple juice
¾ cup unsweetened orange juice
¼ cup currants
1½ tablespoons brown sugar
1 tablespoon cornstarch
¼ teaspoon ground cloves

Prick squash several times with a fork. Place squash on two layers of paper towels. Microwave, uncovered, at HIGH 5 to 6 minutes or until slightly tender. Let cool. Cut ends off squash; discard seeds and ends. Slice squash into 1-inch-thick slices, and arrange squash slices in a 13- x 9- x 2-inch baking dish.

Combine pineapple juice and remaining 5 ingredients; stir well. Pour over squash slices. Bake, uncovered, at 350° for 35 minutes or until squash is tender, brushing squash often with glaze. Yield: 4 servings.

PER SERVING: 164 CALORIES (3% FROM FAT)
FAT 0.6G (SATURATED FAT 0.0G)
PROTEIN 2.2G CARBOHYDRATE 41.1G
CHOLESTEROL 0MG SODIUM 12MG

Fruit-Glazed Acorn Squash

Spinach-Topped Tomatoes

SPINACH-TOPPED TOMATOES

Serve these tasty tomatoes with slices of grilled pork or beef.

12 (½-inch-thick) tomato slices
Vegetable cooking spray
1 (10-ounce) package frozen chopped spinach
⅓ cup grated Parmesan cheese, divided
⅔ cup Italian-seasoned breadcrumbs
½ cup thinly sliced green onions
½ cup fat-free egg substitute
1 tablespoon skim milk
12 pimiento strips (about 1 tablespoon)
¼ teaspoon freshly ground pepper

Arrange tomato slices in a 13- x 9- x 2-inch baking dish coated with cooking spray; set aside.

Cook spinach according to package directions, omitting salt; drain well. Press spinach between paper towels to remove excess moisture. Combine spinach, ¼ cup Parmesan cheese, and next 4 ingredients; stir well.

Spoon 2 tablespoons spinach mixture over each tomato slice; sprinkle evenly with remaining Parmesan cheese. Top each tomato slice with 2 pimiento strips in a crisscross pattern; sprinkle with pepper.

Bake tomatoes at 375° for 10 to 12 minutes or until thoroughly heated and lightly browned. Yield: 6 servings.

PER SERVING: 86 CALORIES (13% FROM FAT)
FAT 1.2G (SATURATED FAT 0.4G)
PROTEIN 6.2G CARBOHYDRATE 14.3G
CHOLESTEROL 1MG SODIUM 360MG

Fiesta Spanish Rice

FIESTA SPANISH RICE

Spanish rice is a traditional accompaniment to tacos, fajitas, and other Mexican fare.

Vegetable cooking spray
¼ cup chopped onion
2 cloves garlic, minced
1 (14½-ounce) can no-salt-added whole
    tomatoes, undrained and chopped
1 (14¼-ounce) can no-salt-added beef broth
1 (4.5-ounce) can chopped green chiles,
    undrained
1½ teaspoons chili powder
⅛ teaspoon salt
Dash of hot sauce
1 cup long-grain rice, uncooked

Coat a large saucepan with cooking spray; place over medium-high heat until hot. Add onion and garlic; sauté until crisp-tender.

Stir in tomatoes and next 5 ingredients; bring mixture to a boil.

Stir in rice. Cover, reduce heat, and simmer 20 to 25 minutes or until liquid is absorbed and rice is tender. Yield: 6 (½-cup) servings.

PER SERVING: 145 CALORIES (3% FROM FAT)
FAT 0.5G (SATURATED FAT 0.1G)
PROTEIN 3.5G   CARBOHYDRATE 31.1G
CHOLESTEROL 0MG   SODIUM 143MG

CONFETTI RICE

¾ cup long-grain rice, uncooked
2 tablespoons reduced-calorie margarine
1 cup sliced green onions
1 teaspoon ground cumin
½ teaspoon dried oregano
¼ teaspoon salt
2 cloves garlic, minced
1 medium-size green pepper, seeded and
    chopped
1 medium-size sweet red pepper, seeded and
    chopped
¼ cup water
1 (10½-ounce) can low-sodium chicken broth

Place a large nonstick skillet over medium-high heat until hot. Add rice; cook 3 to 4 minutes or until lightly browned. Remove rice from skillet, and set aside.

Melt margarine in skillet over medium-high heat. Add green onions and next 6 ingredients; sauté 3 minutes. Add rice, water, and broth. Bring mixture to a boil; cover, reduce heat, and simmer 20 minutes or until liquid is absorbed and rice is tender. Yield: 6 (¾-cup) servings.

PER SERVING: 126 CALORIES (23% FROM FAT)
FAT 3.2G (SATURATED FAT 0.4G)
PROTEIN 2.8G   CARBOHYDRATE 22.1G
CHOLESTEROL 0MG   SODIUM 156MG

PIZZERIA PASTA

Pizzeria Pasta is a real family-pleaser that's easy on the cook. It uses fresh cheese tortellini, which cooks in just five minutes.

1 (9-ounce) package refrigerated fresh cheese
    tortellini, uncooked
Vegetable cooking spray
½ cup chopped green pepper
⅓ cup chopped onion
1 (8-ounce) can no-salt-added tomato sauce
¼ cup sliced ripe olives
1 teaspoon dried Italian seasoning
⅛ teaspoon garlic powder

Cook pasta according to package directions, omitting salt and fat; drain well. Place in a serving bowl; keep warm.

Coat a medium nonstick skillet with cooking spray. Place over medium-high heat until hot. Add green pepper and onion; sauté until tender.

Stir in tomato sauce and remaining 3 ingredients. Cook over medium-low heat until thoroughly heated, stirring occasionally. Add tomato mixture to pasta; toss gently. Serve immediately. Yield: 6 (½-cup) servings.

PER SERVING: 168 CALORIES (23% FROM FAT)
FAT 4.2G (SATURATED FAT 1.2G)
PROTEIN 7.2G   CARBOHYDRATE 24.9G
CHOLESTEROL 20MG   SODIUM 246MG

Quick After-School Pizza (recipe on page 117)

SUPER SNACKS

"*M*om, I'm hungry! May I have a snack?"
It's so easy to let children open a bag of chips or candy
bars, although we know neither is a good choice. As an
alternative, try the tasty snacks in this chapter—they're
easy to prepare and high in nutritional value. Several
refreshing beverages appear on pages 109 through 112.
Ingredients such as fruit, milk, yogurt, and ice cream make
up these drinks that will satisfy those midafternoon hunger
attacks.

Beginning on page 113, you'll find an assortment of
quick pick-me-ups, including a snack mix, miniature pizza,
and fruit kabobs. There's also a carrot-raisin cake on page
121 that's rich with vitamins. Your kids will never guess
that such a delicious snack could be called healthy.

And don't be fooled—the recipes in this chapter are
just as satisfying for adults as they are for the young ones.

Apple and Lemon Sparkle

APPLE AND LEMON SPARKLE

1 (6-ounce) can unsweetened frozen apple
    juice concentrate, thawed and undiluted
1 (6-ounce) can frozen lemonade concentrate,
    thawed and undiluted
1 (33.8-ounce) bottle seltzer water, chilled
1 medium-size Red Delicious apple,
    quartered and thinly sliced
½ medium lemon, thinly sliced
24 Apple-Lemonade Cubes

Combine first 3 ingredients in a large pitcher; stir well. Stir in apple and lemon slices. To serve, place 4 Apple-Lemonade Cubes into each of six glasses. Pour 1 cup apple-lemon mixture into each glass. Yield: 6 servings.

Apple-Lemonade Cubes
1 (6-ounce) can unsweetened frozen apple
    juice concentrate, thawed and undiluted
1 (6-ounce) can frozen lemonade concentrate,
    thawed and undiluted
4½ cups water

Combine all ingredients in a large pitcher; stir well. Pour 2 tablespoons mixture into each of 56 ice cube tray compartments; freeze until firm. Yield: 56 cubes.

PER SERVING: 158 CALORIES (2% FROM FAT)
FAT 0.3G (SATURATED FAT 0.0G)
PROTEIN 0.4G CARBOHYDRATE 40.2G
CHOLESTEROL 0MG SODIUM 46MG

PINEAPPLE PLEASURE

1½ cups sliced strawberries, chilled
1¼ cups sliced banana
1¼ cups unsweetened pineapple juice, chilled
1 cup unsweetened orange juice, chilled
1 cup crushed ice
2 tablespoons honey

Place all ingredients in container of an electric blender; cover and process until smooth. Serve immediately. Yield: 5 (1-cup) servings.

PER SERVING: 131 CALORIES (3% FROM FAT)
FAT 0.4G (SATURATED FAT 0.1G)
PROTEIN 1.2G CARBOHYDRATE 32.9G
CHOLESTEROL 0MG SODIUM 2MG

SPARKLING STRAWBERRY LEMONADE

1 (12-ounce) package frozen unsweetened
    strawberries, thawed
2 (12-ounce) cans frozen pink lemonade
    concentrate, thawed and undiluted
2 cups water
4 cups berry-flavored sparkling mineral water,
    chilled
Lemon slices (optional)

Place strawberries in container of an electric blender; cover and process until smooth, stopping once to scrape down sides. Pour strawberry puree through a wire-mesh strainer into a large freezer-proof container, discarding pulp and seeds. Add lemonade and water to container; stir well. Cover and freeze 4 hours or until slushy.

To serve, transfer lemonade mixture to a large pitcher or a small punch bowl. Stir in mineral water, and serve immediately. Garnish with lemon slices, if desired. Yield: 10 (1-cup) servings.

PER SERVING: 135 CALORIES (1% FROM FAT)
FAT 0.2G (SATURATED FAT 0.0G)
PROTEIN 0.3G CARBOHYDRATE 35.1G
CHOLESTEROL 0MG SODIUM 23MG

FROSTY RASPBERRY SIPPER

1¼ cups fresh raspberries
1¼ cups unsweetened white grape juice
1½ cups raspberry sherbet
¼ cup water
1 tablespoon lemon juice
10 ice cubes
Fresh mint sprigs (optional)

Combine raspberries and grape juice in container of an electric blender; cover and process until smooth, stopping once to scrape down sides. Strain mixture through several layers of dampened cheesecloth, reserving liquid and discarding solids.

Combine reserved liquid, sherbet, water, and lemon juice in blender container; cover and process until smooth. Add ice cubes; cover and process until frothy. Serve immediately. Garnish with fresh mint sprigs, if desired. Yield: 4 (1-cup) servings.

PER SERVING: 151 CALORIES (5% FROM FAT)
FAT 0.9G (SATURATED FAT 0.0G)
PROTEIN 1.4G   CARBOHYDRATE 35.9G
CHOLESTEROL 0MG   SODIUM 53MG

Frosty Raspberry Sipper

CREAMY ORANGE FROST

1 (12-ounce) can frozen orange juice
    concentrate
2 (12-ounce) cans evaporated skimmed milk,
    chilled
8 ice cubes

Combine half each of all ingredients in container of an electric blender; cover and process until smooth. Repeat procedure with remaining ingredients. Serve immediately. Yield: 6 (1-cup) servings.

PER SERVING: 179 CALORIES (2% FROM FAT)
FAT 0.3G (SATURATED FAT 0.2G)
PROTEIN 9.9G   CARBOHYDRATE 35.0G
CHOLESTEROL 5MG   SODIUM 132MG

CREAMY RASPBERRY FROST
Substitute 2 (10-ounce) packages frozen raspberries in light syrup for orange juice, and add ½ cup powdered sugar. Yield: 8 (1-cup) servings.

PER SERVING: 169 CALORIES (2% FROM FAT)
FAT 0.3G (SATURATED FAT 0.1G)
PROTEIN 6.9G   CARBOHYDRATE 36.0G
CHOLESTEROL 3MG   SODIUM 99MG

CREAMY STRAWBERRY FROST
Substitute 2 (10-ounce) packages frozen strawberries in light syrup for orange juice, and add ½ cup powdered sugar. Yield: 8 (1-cup) servings.

PER SERVING: 151 CALORIES (2% FROM FAT)
FAT 0.3G (SATURATED FAT 0.1G)
PROTEIN 6.8G   CARBOHYDRATE 32.0G
CHOLESTEROL 3MG   SODIUM 99MG

Strawberry Smoothies

MIDNIGHT MALTS
(pictured on page 114)

1 cup vanilla low-fat ice cream
1 cup 1% low-fat milk
2 tablespoons chocolate malted milk powder
¼ teaspoons vanilla extract
⅛ teaspoon ground cinnamon

Combine first 4 ingredients in container of an electric blender; cover and process until smooth. Pour into glasses; sprinkle with cinnamon. Serve immediately. Yield: 2 (1-cup) servings.

PER SERVING: 180 CALORIES (24% FROM FAT)
FAT 4.8G (SATURATED FAT 3.0G)
PROTEIN 7.7G CARBOHYDRATE 26.8G
CHOLESTEROL 14MG SODIUM 153MG

CHOCOLATE WAFER MALTS

1 quart vanilla nonfat frozen yogurt, softened
1 cup 1% low-fat chocolate milk
10 chocolate wafer cookies, coarsely crumbled

Combine yogurt and milk in container of an electric blender; cover and process until smooth, stopping once to scrape down sides. Stir in cookie crumbs. Pour into glasses, and serve immediately. Yield: 4 (1-cup) servings.

PER SERVING: 260 CALORIES (11% FROM FAT)
FAT 3.3G (SATURATED FAT 1.1G)
PROTEIN 9.7G CARBOHYDRATE 50.2G
CHOLESTEROL 12MG SODIUM 208MG

STRAWBERRY SMOOTHIES

1 cup nonfat buttermilk
1 cup unsweetened orange juice
1 cup sliced fresh strawberries
2 tablespoons sugar

Combine all ingredients in container of an electric blender; cover and process until smooth. Serve immediately. Yield: 3 (1-cup) servings.

PER SERVING: 115 CALORIES (4% FROM FAT)
FAT 0.5G (SATURATED FAT 0.3G)
PROTEIN 3.9G CARBOHYDRATE 24.9G
CHOLESTEROL 3MG SODIUM 91MG

PEPPERMINT COOLER

¾ cup vanilla low-fat ice cream
¾ cup skim milk
7 ice cubes
4 hard round peppermint candies

Combine all ingredients in container of an electric blender; cover and process until smooth. Serve immediately. Yield: 2 (1-cup) servings.

PER SERVING: 153 CALORIES (14% FROM FAT)
FAT 2.3G (SATURATED FAT 1.4G)
PROTEIN 5.0G   CARBOHYDRATE 29.4G
CHOLESTEROL 9MG   SODIUM 95MG

CARAMEL HOT COCOA

1 tablespoon sugar
1 tablespoon unsweetened cocoa
1¾ cups skim milk
2 tablespoons caramel-flavored topping

Combine sugar and cocoa in a small saucepan; stir in skim milk and caramel topping. Cook over medium heat, stirring constantly, until mixture is thoroughly heated and caramel topping dissolves. Serve immediately. Yield: 2 (1-cup) servings.

PER SERVING: 163 CALORIES (4% FROM FAT)
FAT 0.7G (SATURATED FAT 0.5G)
PROTEIN 8.4G   CARBOHYDRATE 31.5G
CHOLESTEROL 4MG   SODIUM 150MG

CINNAMON CREAM HOT COCOA

3 cups skim milk
2 (3-inch) sticks cinnamon
¼ cup unsweetened cocoa
3 tablespoons sugar
⅓ cup marshmallow cream
1½ teaspoons vanilla extract
¼ teaspoon almond extract
Cinnamon sticks (optional)

Place milk and 2 sticks cinnamon in a medium saucepan. Bring to a boil over medium heat, stirring occasionally. Remove from heat, and cool 10 minutes. Remove and discard cinnamon sticks.

Combine cocoa and sugar; stir well. Add to milk mixture, and stir well. Stir in marshmallow cream. Cook over medium heat, stirring constantly with a wire whisk, until heated. Remove from heat; stir in flavorings. Pour into mugs. Garnish with cinnamon sticks, if desired. Yield: 4 (¾-cup) servings.

PER SERVING: 171 CALORIES (6% FROM FAT)
FAT 1.1G (SATURATED FAT 0.7G)
PROTEIN 7.9G   CARBOHYDRATE 31.3G
CHOLESTEROL 4MG   SODIUM 101MG

CRISPY POTATO SKIN SNACKS

4 (8-ounce) baking potatoes
1½ tablespoons chili powder
2 teaspoons paprika
1 teaspoon ground cumin
½ teaspoon garlic powder
½ teaspoon onion powder
½ teaspoon dried oregano
¼ teaspoon salt
¼ teaspoon ground red pepper
Butter-flavored vegetable cooking spray
½ cup (2 ounces) finely shredded reduced-fat sharp Cheddar cheese

Scrub potatoes; prick each several times with a fork. Bake at 400° for 45 minutes. Let cool.

Combine chili powder and next 7 ingredients, stirring well; set aside.

Cut potatoes in half lengthwise. Scoop out pulp, leaving ¼-inch-thick shells. Reserve pulp for another use. Cut each potato shell into 4 wedges. Coat wedges with cooking spray; sprinkle with chili powder mixture and cheese. Bake at 400° for 10 minutes or until crisp. Yield: 32 snacks.

PER SNACK: 21 CALORIES (21% FROM FAT)
FAT 0.5G (SATURATED FAT 0.2G)
PROTEIN 0.9G   CARBOHYDRATE 3.5G
CHOLESTEROL 1MG   SODIUM 36MG

Cheesy Chili Dip

CHEESY CHILI DIP

1 cup 1% low-fat cottage cheese
¼ cup (1 ounce) shredded reduced-fat sharp
   Cheddar cheese
¼ cup chopped onion
¼ cup plain nonfat yogurt
¼ cup reduced-calorie ketchup
1 tablespoon chopped fresh parsley
¾ teaspoon chili powder
¼ teaspoon garlic powder
⅛ teaspoon ground cumin

Position knife blade in food processor bowl; add cottage cheese. Process until smooth, stopping once to scrape down sides. Add Cheddar cheese and remaining ingredients; process until smooth, stopping once to scrape down sides. Serve with raw vegetables. Yield: 1⅔ cups.

PER TABLESPOON: 12 CALORIES (23% FROM FAT)
FAT 0.3G (SATURATED FAT 0.2G)
PROTEIN 1.5G   CARBOHYDRATE 0.8G
CHOLESTEROL 1MG   SODIUM 45MG

Moonlight Snaps and Midnight Malts (recipe on page 111)

MOONLIGHT SNAPS

2 tablespoons grated Parmesan cheese
2 tablespoons water
2 teaspoons dried oregano
1 teaspoon olive oil
⅛ to ¼ teaspoon ground red pepper
2 large cloves garlic, crushed
2 (6-inch) whole wheat pita bread rounds

Combine first 6 ingredients in a small bowl; stir well. Split each pita round in half horizontally.

Brush Parmesan cheese mixture over interior side of each pita half; cut each pita half into 8 wedges. Place wedges in a single layer on a baking sheet.

Bake pita wedges at 375° for 12 minutes or until crisp and lightly browned. Cool on a wire rack. Yield: 4 servings.

PER SERVING: 79 CALORIES (30% FROM FAT)
FAT 2.6G (SATURATED FAT 0.8G)
PROTEIN 3.5G CARBOHYDRATE 11.5G
CHOLESTEROL 3MG SODIUM 160MG

PARMESAN-CORNMEAL STICKS

1 cup all-purpose flour
½ cup yellow cornmeal
⅓ cup grated Parmesan cheese
2 tablespoons sesame seeds, toasted
¾ teaspoon baking soda
¼ teaspoon salt
⅛ teaspoon ground red pepper
½ cup skim milk
1 tablespoon vegetable oil
Vegetable cooking spray

Combine first 7 ingredients in a large bowl; stir well. Combine milk and oil; add to dry ingredients, stirring just until dry ingredients are moistened.

Turn dough out onto a lightly floured surface; roll to an 8-inch square. Using a pizza cutter, cut dough into 4 (4-inch) squares; cut each square into 8 (½-inch-wide) strips. Arrange strips on a baking sheet coated with cooking spray. Bake at 375° for 20 minutes. Cool on a wire rack. Yield: 8 servings.

PER SERVING: 134 CALORIES (30% FROM FAT)
FAT 4.4G (SATURATED FAT 1.2G)
PROTEIN 4.7G CARBOHYDRATE 18.8G
CHOLESTEROL 3MG SODIUM 222MG

Parmesan-Cornmeal Sticks and Peanut Butter-Granola Munchies (recipe on page 120)

MEXICAN CORN STRIPS

1 teaspoon chili powder
¼ teaspoon salt
¼ teaspoon ground cumin
⅛ teaspoon garlic powder
⅛ teaspoon onion powder
12 (6-inch) corn tortillas
Butter-flavored vegetable cooking spray

Combine first 5 ingredients in a large heavy-duty, zip-top plastic bag; set aside. Coat 1 side of each tortilla with cooking spray; cut each tortilla into 8 strips. Place strips in bag; seal bag, and shake to coat.

Place tortilla strips in a single layer on baking sheets. Bake at 350° for 15 minutes or until crisp. Cool on a wire rack. Yield: 8 servings.

PER SERVING: 105 CALORIES (17% FROM FAT)
FAT 2.0G (SATURATED FAT 0.2G)
PROTEIN 3.2G CARBOHYDRATE 19.4G
CHOLESTEROL 0MG SODIUM 156MG

SUGAR AND SPICE SNACK MIX

6 cups crispy corn cereal squares
2 cups miniature pretzels
3 egg whites, lightly beaten
1⅓ cups sugar
2 teaspoons ground cinnamon
1 teaspoon orange extract
Vegetable cooking spray

Combine cereal and pretzels in a large bowl. Combine egg whites and next 3 ingredients, stirring well with a wire whisk; pour over cereal mixture, tossing gently to coat.

Spread cereal mixture in a 15- x 10- x 1-inch jellyroll pan coated with cooking spray. Bake at 275° for 50 minutes or until crisp, stirring every 15 minutes. Cool. Yield: 36 (¼-cup) servings.

PER SERVING: 61 CALORIES (3% FROM FAT)
FAT 0.2G (SATURATED FAT 0.0G)
PROTEIN 0.8G CARBOHYDRATE 13.8G
CHOLESTEROL 0MG SODIUM 83MG

Ham and Cheese Sandwich Stacks and Fudgy Chocolate Cones (recipe on page 120)

HAM AND CHEESE SANDWICH STACKS

¼ cup reduced-calorie mayonnaise
1 teaspoon prepared mustard
⅛ teaspoon onion powder
½ cup (2 ounces) shredded part-skim
    mozzarella cheese
½ cup (2 ounces) shredded reduced-fat sharp
    Cheddar cheese
¾ cup finely chopped lean, lower-salt ham
10 (½-ounce) slices very thinly sliced whole
    wheat bread
10 (½-ounce) slices very thinly sliced white
    bread
30 small salted pretzel sticks

Combine first 3 ingredients in a medium bowl;
stir well. Add cheeses and ham; stir well.

Stack 2 slices whole wheat bread and 2 slices
white bread, alternating whole wheat and white
slices. Spread about 1 tablespoon ham mixture
between each layer. Repeat procedure with
remaining bread and ham mixture. Cut each sandwich stack into 3 rectangles. Cut each rectangle in
half crosswise, making 6 tiny sandwiches. Spear
each with a pretzel stick. Yield: 30 snacks.

Note: To make ahead, assemble sandwiches, and
place on a serving platter. Cover with damp paper
towels and plastic wrap; chill. Spear each sandwich
with a pretzel stick just before serving.

PER SNACK: 50 CALORIES (29% FROM FAT)
FAT 1.6G (SATURATED FAT 0.6G)
PROTEIN 2.8G   CARBOHYDRATE 6.3G
CHOLESTEROL 5MG   SODIUM 368MG

TOMATO-CHEESE MELTS

2 onion bagels, each sliced in half
4 (¼-inch-thick) slices tomato
¼ cup (1 ounce) shredded reduced-fat
    Cheddar cheese
¼ cup crumbled feta cheese
Ground red pepper (optional)

Place bagel halves on a large ungreased baking sheet; top each with a tomato slice. Sprinkle evenly with cheeses. Sprinkle with ground red pepper, if desired. Broil 3 inches from heat (with electric oven door partially opened) 3 minutes or until cheeses melt. Serve immediately. Yield: 4 servings.

PER SERVING: 193 CALORIES (18% FROM FAT)
FAT 3.8G (SATURATED FAT 2.0G)
PROTEIN 9.0G CARBOHYDRATE 30.5G
CHOLESTEROL 11MG SODIUM 418MG

QUICK AFTER-SCHOOL PIZZA

(pictured on page 106)

1 (8-inch) flour tortilla
Vegetable cooking spray
2½ tablespoons no-salt-added tomato sauce
2 teaspoons minced onion
¼ teaspoon dried oregano
¼ cup (1 ounce) shredded part-skim
    mozzarella cheese
2 teaspoons grated Parmesan cheese

Place tortilla on a baking sheet coated with cooking spray. Bake at 400° for 3 minutes. Turn tortilla; spread tomato sauce evenly over tortilla, leaving a ½-inch border around edge. Sprinkle with onion, oregano, and cheeses. Bake 5 minutes or until golden. Cut into 4 wedges. Yield: 4 snacks.

PER SNACK: 62 CALORIES (33% FROM FAT)
FAT 2.3G (SATURATED FAT 0.9G)
PROTEIN 3.1G CARBOHYDRATE 7.1G
CHOLESTEROL 5MG SODIUM 102MG

SPICY PIZZA SNACKS

Vegetable cooking spray
3 ounces freshly ground raw turkey
1 tablespoon finely chopped green pepper
1 teaspoon dried onion flakes
1 teaspoon low-sodium Worcestershire sauce
½ teaspoon pepper
¼ teaspoon rubbed sage
¼ cup fat-free spaghetti sauce
6 miniature English muffins, split
6 ounces part-skim mozzarella cheese, cut into
    24 slices

Coat a nonstick skillet with cooking spray; place over medium-high heat until hot. Add turkey and next 5 ingredients. Cook until turkey is browned, stirring until it crumbles; drain, if necessary, and return to skillet. Add spaghetti sauce; cook until heated.

Place muffin halves, cut sides up, on an ungreased baking sheet; broil 5½ inches from heat (with electric oven door partially opened) until lightly toasted.

Spoon 1 tablespoon turkey mixture onto each muffin half; top each serving with 2 slices cheese. Broil 5½ inches from heat (with electric oven door partially opened) until cheese melts. Serve warm. Yield: 12 snacks.

PER SNACK: 102 CALORIES (30% FROM FAT)
FAT 3.4G (SATURATED FAT 1.7G)
PROTEIN 6.4G CARBOHYDRATE 11.2G
CHOLESTEROL 12MG SODIUM 184MG

BERRY POPS

*Each of these frozen strawberry pops has
less than one gram of fat.*

1 envelope unflavored gelatin
1 cup peach nectar
2 cups vanilla low-fat yogurt
1 teaspoon vanilla extract
2½ cups frozen unsweetened strawberries,
    thawed
8 (3-ounce) paper cups
8 wooden sticks

Sprinkle gelatin over peach nectar in a small
saucepan; let stand 1 minute. Cook over low heat,
stirring until gelatin dissolves, about 2 minutes.
Remove from heat; add yogurt and vanilla, stirring
with a wire whisk until smooth.

Mash strawberries; add to yogurt mixture. Spoon
strawberry mixture evenly into paper cups. Cover
tops of cups with aluminum foil, and insert a
wooden stick through foil into center of each cup.
Freeze until firm. To serve, remove aluminum foil;
peel cup from pop. Yield: 8 pops.

PER POP: 86 CALORIES (8% FROM FAT)
FAT 0.8G (SATURATED FAT 0.5G)
PROTEIN 3.8G   CARBOHYDRATE 16.4G
CHOLESTEROL 3MG   SODIUM 42MG

Quick Snacks

Here are some simple dip ideas for fresh
fruit that children are sure to love.
• Mix peanut butter with honey; add
raisins, and use as a dip for apple wedges.
• Combine vanilla low-fat yogurt, orange
marmalade, and a dash of cinnamon to serve
with peach slices.
• Combine peanut butter and a small
amount of orange low-fat yogurt to make a
dip for fresh fruit or graham crackers.
• Stir brown sugar and toasted coconut into
vanilla yogurt; serve with pineapple spears.

FRUIT KABOBS WITH YOGURT-PINEAPPLE DIP

2 medium-size red apples
2 medium pears
2 tablespoons lemon juice
42 unsweetened pineapple chunks
42 seedless red and green grapes (about ½
    pound)
42 fresh strawberries, hulled
Yogurt-Pineapple Dip

Cut each apple and pear into 21 bite-size pieces.
Combine apple, pear, and lemon juice, tossing
gently.

Thread apple, pear, pineapple, grapes, and strawberries alternately onto 42 (6-inch) skewers. Serve
each kabob with about 1 tablespoon plus 1 teaspoon Yogurt-Pineapple Dip. Yield: 42 snacks.

YOGURT-PINEAPPLE DIP

1 (8-ounce) package reduced-fat cream cheese,
    softened
2 (8-ounce) cartons vanilla low-fat yogurt
1 teaspoon lemon juice
½ teaspoon grated orange rind
⅛ teaspoon coconut extract
1 (8-ounce) can unsweetened crushed
    pineapple, drained

Beat cream cheese at medium speed of an
electric mixer until light and fluffy; add yogurt
and next 3 ingredients. Beat until smooth. Stir in
crushed pineapple. Cover and chill thoroughly.
Yield: 3½ cups.

PER SNACK: 42 CALORIES (26% FROM FAT)
FAT 1.2G (SATURATED FAT 0.7G)
PROTEIN 1.3G   CARBOHYDRATE 7.3G
CHOLESTEROL 4MG   SODIUM 38MG

Fruit Kabobs with Yogurt-Pineapple Dip

PEANUT BUTTER-GRANOLA MUNCHIES
(pictured on page 115)

2 tablespoons margarine
2 tablespoons creamy peanut butter
3 cups miniature marshmallows (about 5½ ounces)
2½ cups low-fat granola with raisins
Vegetable cooking spray

Combine margarine and peanut butter in a saucepan; cook over low heat until margarine and peanut butter melt, stirring often. Add marshmallows; cover and cook 5 minutes or until marshmallows melt, stirring occasionally. Remove from heat, and add granola. Working rapidly, toss gently; spread mixture into bottom of an 8½- x 4½- x 3-inch loafpan coated with cooking spray. Cool in pan.

Remove from pan; cut in half lengthwise, and then slice each half crosswise into 8 bars. Yield: 16 bars.

PER BAR: 112 CALORIES (28% FROM FAT)
FAT 3.5G (SATURATED FAT 0.5G)
PROTEIN 2.3G CARBOHYDRATE 19.8G
CHOLESTEROL 0MG SODIUM 61MG

CHOCOLATE-NUT POPCORN CLUSTERS

1½ cups sugar
½ cup water
⅓ cup light-colored corn syrup
2 tablespoons unsweetened cocoa
1 teaspoon vanilla extract
½ teaspoon baking soda
¼ teaspoon salt
7 cups popped corn (popped without salt or fat)
½ cup coarsely chopped unsalted dry-roasted peanuts
Vegetable cooking spray

Combine first 4 ingredients in a Dutch oven; stir until smooth. Bring to a boil over medium-high heat, and cook until mixture reaches hard crack stage (310°), stirring occasionally. Remove from heat; stir in vanilla, baking soda, and salt. Add popped corn and peanuts. Working rapidly, toss gently; spread onto a baking sheet coated with cooking spray. Cool; break into pieces. Store in an airtight container. Yield: 16 (½-cup) servings.

PER SERVING: 133 CALORIES (17% FROM FAT)
FAT 2.5G (SATURATED FAT 0.4G)
PROTEIN 1.7G CARBOHYDRATE 27.0G
CHOLESTEROL 0MG SODIUM 72MG

FUDGY CHOCOLATE CONES
(pictured on page 116)

12 colored cake cones with flat bottoms
4 egg whites
¼ teaspoon cream of tartar
⅔ cup sugar
1½ teaspoons vanilla extract
2 tablespoons unsweetened cocoa
3 tablespoons semisweet chocolate mini-morsels
1 tablespoon multicolored sugar sprinkles

Cut 12 (15- x 12-inch) sheets of aluminum foil. Wrap 1 sheet loosely around each cone. Fit foil and cone into each of 12 muffin cups; set aside.

Beat egg whites and cream of tartar at high speed of an electric mixer until soft peaks form. Gradually add sugar, 1 tablespoon at a time, beating until stiff peaks form. (Do not underbeat.) Beat in vanilla. Sift cocoa over egg white mixture; gently fold cocoa and mini-morsels into mixture until combined.

Spoon egg white mixture into a heavy-duty, zip-top plastic bag; seal bag. Snip a corner off bag; pipe mixture evenly into cones. Top each with ¼ teaspoon sprinkles. Bake at 325° for 25 minutes. Turn off oven; cool in closed oven 1 hour. Remove cones from oven; cool completely. Yield: 12 servings.

PER SERVING: 110 CALORIES (13% FROM FAT)
FAT 1.6G (SATURATED FAT 0.8G)
PROTEIN 2.4G CARBOHYDRATE 22.0G
CHOLESTEROL 0MG SODIUM 43MG

Carrot-Raisin Snack Cake

CARROT-RAISIN SNACK CAKE

⅓ cup margarine, softened
½ cup firmly packed dark brown sugar
⅔ cup unsweetened applesauce
½ cup fat-free egg substitute
1½ cups sifted cake flour
1½ teaspoons baking powder
¼ teaspoon salt
1 teaspoon ground cinnamon
1 cup finely shredded carrot
½ cup raisins
Vegetable cooking spray
1 tablespoon powdered sugar

Beat margarine at medium speed of an electric mixer until creamy; gradually add brown sugar, beating well. Add applesauce and egg substitute, and beat well.

Combine flour and next 3 ingredients; add to margarine mixture, stirring well. Stir in carrot and raisins.

Pour batter into an 8-inch square pan coated with cooking spray. Bake at 350° for 25 minutes or until a wooden pick inserted in center comes out clean. Cool in pan on a wire rack. Sift powdered sugar over cooled cake. Cut into squares. Yield: 9 squares.

PER SQUARE: 218 CALORIES (29% FROM FAT)
FAT 7.0G (SATURATED FAT 1.4G)
PROTEIN 3.3G   CARBOHYDRATE 36.6G
CHOLESTEROL 0MG   SODIUM 174MG

Lemon Cream Pie (recipe on page 134)

WINNING DESSERTS

You're trying to adopt a healthier way of eating for your family. But while you may have found it fairly easy to cut the fat from main dishes and vegetables, wouldn't you love to indulge in a piece of sinfully rich chocolate cake?

Delight your family members today by welcoming them home with a slice of freshly baked Chocolate-Buttermilk Pound Cake featured on page 126. If cookies are what they fancy, turn to pages 128 through 132 for some new ideas. Rounding out the chapter are recipes for delicious pies, puddings, and ice cream dishes.

The adults in your home will be amazed that these desserts are so low in fat and calories. And everyone, from the youngest up, will be thrilled with the taste.

BLUEBERRY BUCKLE

½ cup sugar
3 tablespoons stick margarine, softened
½ cup low-fat sour cream
½ teaspoon grated orange rind
1 egg
½ cup all-purpose flour
¼ teaspoon baking soda
⅛ teaspoon salt
¼ cup yellow cornmeal
3 egg whites
¼ cup sugar
2 cups fresh or frozen blueberries, thawed and drained
Vegetable cooking spray
1 tablespoon stick margarine
½ cup sifted powdered sugar
1 tablespoon water
1 teaspoon vanilla extract

Combine ½ cup sugar and 3 tablespoons margarine in a large bowl; beat at medium speed of an electric mixer until light and fluffy (about 5 minutes). Add sour cream, orange rind, and egg; beat until well blended. Combine flour and next 3 ingredients; add to sour cream mixture, beating just until dry ingredients are moistened. Set aside.

Beat egg whites at high speed until foamy. Gradually add ¼ cup sugar, 1 tablespoon at a time, beating until stiff peaks form. Gently fold into sour cream mixture; fold in blueberries.

Spoon batter into a 9-inch round cakepan coated with cooking spray. Bake at 350° for 40 minutes or until cake springs back when lightly touched in center. Cool in pan on a wire rack 15 minutes; remove from pan.

Place 1 tablespoon margarine in a small saucepan; cook over medium heat until browned. Remove from heat; cool slightly. Stir in powdered sugar, water, and vanilla; drizzle over cake. To serve, cut into wedges. Yield: 8 servings.

Note: Although buckles traditionally call for berries, you can use fruits like peaches and pears.

PER SERVING: 253 CALORIES (31% FROM FAT)
FAT 8.6G (SATURATED FAT 2.5G)
PROTEIN 3.9G CARBOHYDRATE 41.2G
CHOLESTEROL 33MG SODIUM 180MG

CARAMEL-PINEAPPLE UPSIDE-DOWN CAKE

1 (15¼-ounce) can unsweetened pineapple slices, undrained
½ cup sugar
2½ tablespoons water
¼ cup stick margarine, divided
Vegetable cooking spray
9 maraschino cherry halves
½ cup firmly packed brown sugar
1 egg
1 egg white
1¼ cups all-purpose flour
½ teaspoon baking soda
½ teaspoon baking powder
¼ teaspoon salt
½ cup nonfat buttermilk
½ teaspoon vanilla extract

Drain pineapple, reserving ¼ cup juice. Set aside 5 pineapple slices, reserving remaining slices for another use.

Combine ½ cup sugar and water in a small heavy saucepan. Place over medium-low heat, and cook 6 minutes or until sugar dissolves. (Do not stir.) Cover, increase heat to medium, and cook 1 minute. Uncover and cook 5 additional minutes or until sugar mixture is amber or golden.

Remove from heat, and let stand 1 minute. Add 1 tablespoon margarine, stirring until margarine melts. Gradually add ¼ cup reserved pineapple juice, stirring constantly. (The caramelized sugar will harden and stick to spoon.) Place over medium heat; cook, stirring constantly, 3 minutes or until caramel melts and mixture is smooth.

Pour caramel mixture into a 9-inch round cakepan coated with cooking spray. Place 1 pineapple slice in center of cakepan; cut remaining 4 pineapple slices in half, and arrange slices spoke-fashion around whole slice in center. Place a cherry half in center of each pineapple slice; set aside.

Beat remaining 3 tablespoons margarine in a large mixing bowl at medium speed of an electric mixer until creamy; gradually add brown sugar, beating well (about 5 minutes). Add egg and egg white, and beat well.

Caramel-Pineapple Upside-Down Cake

Combine flour and next 3 ingredients; add to margarine mixture alternately with buttermilk, beginning and ending with flour mixture. Beat at low speed after each addition until blended. Stir in vanilla.

Pour batter evenly over pineapple. Bake at 350° for 30 minutes or until a wooden pick inserted in center comes out clean. Cool in pan 5 minutes; invert cake onto a serving plate. To serve, cut warm cake into wedges. Yield: 10 servings.

PER SERVING: 210 CALORIES (23% FROM FAT)
FAT 5.3G (SATURATED FAT 1.1G)
PROTEIN 3.1G CARBOHYDRATE 37.8G
CHOLESTEROL 22MG SODIUM 199MG

Chocolate-Buttermilk Pound Cake

CHOCOLATE-BUTTERMILK POUND CAKE

¾ cup stick margarine, softened
1½ cups sugar
2 large eggs
2 large egg whites
1½ cups low-fat buttermilk
1 teaspoon baking soda
3½ cups all-purpose flour
1 teaspoon baking powder
¼ teaspoon salt
¾ cup unsweetened cocoa
2 teaspoons vanilla extract
Baking spray with flour
1 teaspoon powdered sugar

Beat margarine at medium speed of an electric mixture until creamy; gradually add 1½ cups sugar, beating mixture well. Add eggs and egg whites,

one at a time, beating mixture well after each addition.

Combine buttermilk and baking soda; stir well. Combine flour and next 3 ingredients; stir mixture well. Add flour mixture to margarine mixture alternately with buttermilk mixture, beginning and ending with flour mixture. Stir in vanilla.

Pour batter into a 12-cup Bundt pan coated with baking spray with flour. Bake at 350° for 45 minutes or until a wooden pick inserted in center comes out clean. Cool in pan 10 minutes on a wire rack; remove from pan. Cool completely on wire rack. Sift powdered sugar over cake. Yield: 18 servings.

PER SERVING: 259 CALORIES (32% FROM FAT)
FAT 9.2G (SATURATED FAT 2.2G)
PROTEIN 5.4G   CARBOHYDRATE 38.4G
CHOLESTEROL 25MG   SODIUM 217MG

CRUMB-TOPPED PEAR-OATMEAL CAKE

1¾ cups all-purpose flour
½ teaspoon baking soda
½ teaspoon baking powder
½ teaspoon salt
½ cup firmly packed brown sugar
1 teaspoon ground cinnamon
¼ teaspoon ground nutmeg
¼ cup nonfat buttermilk
3 tablespoons stick margarine, melted
1 teaspoon vanilla extract
1 egg
1 egg white
1½ cups chopped unpeeled ripe Bosc pear
    (about ¾ pound)
1 cup quick-cooking oats, uncooked and
    divided
Vegetable cooking spray
¼ cup all-purpose flour
3 tablespoons brown sugar
1½ tablespoons stick margarine, melted

Combine first 12 ingredients in a large bowl; beat at medium speed of an electric mixer until well blended. Stir in chopped pear and ½ cup oats. Spread batter into a 9-inch round cakepan coated with cooking spray.

Combine remaining ½ cup oats, ¼ cup flour, 3 tablespoons brown sugar, and 1½ tablespoons margarine, tossing well with a fork until crumbly. Sprinkle over batter. Bake at 350° for 45 minutes or until a wooden pick inserted in center comes out clean. To serve, cut into wedges. Yield: 10 servings.

PER SERVING: 254 CALORIES (23% FROM FAT)
FAT 6.6G (SATURATED FAT 1.3G)
PROTEIN 5.2G CARBOHYDRATE 43.7G
CHOLESTEROL 22MG SODIUM 257MG

CHOCOLATE CUPCAKES

1½ cups all-purpose flour
1 teaspoon baking soda
½ teaspoon salt
½ cup sugar
¼ cup unsweetened cocoa
½ cup unsweetened orange juice
⅓ cup water
3 tablespoons vegetable oil
1 tablespoon white vinegar
1 teaspoon vanilla extract
⅓ cup semisweet chocolate mini-morsels

Combine first 5 ingredients in a large bowl; make a well in center of mixture.

Combine juice and next 4 ingredients; add to flour mixture, stirring just until dry ingredients are moistened. Fold in mini-morsels.

Spoon into foil- or paper-lined muffin pans, filling two-thirds full. Bake at 375° for 15 minutes or until a wooden pick inserted in center comes out clean. Remove from pans immediately; cool on a wire rack. Yield: 10 cupcakes.

PER CUPCAKE: 177 CALORIES (29% FROM FAT)
FAT 5.8G (SATURATED FAT 1.6G)
PROTEIN 2.8G CARBOHYDRATE 28.8G
CHOLESTEROL 0MG SODIUM 245MG

Chocolate Cupcake

Butterscotch Brownies

BUTTERSCOTCH BROWNIES

¼ cup plus 2 tablespoons stick margarine,
 softened
1½ cups firmly packed dark brown sugar
½ cup fat-free egg substitute
2 teaspoons vanilla extract
2 cups all-purpose flour
1 teaspoon baking powder
¼ teaspoon baking soda
½ teaspoon salt
½ cup plus 2 tablespoons butterscotch morsels
Vegetable cooking spray

Beat margarine at medium speed of an electric mixer until creamy; gradually add sugar, beating well. Add egg substitute and vanilla, beating mixture well.

Combine flour and next 3 ingredients. Add to margarine mixture, beating well. Stir in butterscotch morsels.

Spoon mixture into a 13- x 9- x 2-inch pan coated with cooking spray. Bake at 350° for 25 minutes or until a wooden pick inserted in center comes out clean. Remove from oven, and cool completely on a wire rack. Cut into squares. Yield: 2½ dozen.

PER BROWNIE: 115 CALORIES (26% FROM FAT)
FAT 3.3G (SATURATED FAT 0.6G)
PROTEIN 1.4G CARBOHYDRATE 19.8G
CHOLESTEROL 0MG SODIUM 89MG

S'MORE BROWNIES

½ cup sugar
⅓ cup water
2½ tablespoons vegetable oil
½ teaspoon vanilla extract
2 egg whites, lightly beaten
½ cup all-purpose flour
¾ teaspoon baking powder
⅛ teaspoon salt
⅓ cup graham cracker crumbs (about 5 squares)
¼ cup unsweetened cocoa
Vegetable cooking spray
2 cups miniature marshmallows
1 (1-ounce) square semisweet chocolate, grated

Combine first 4 ingredients in a medium bowl. Add egg whites, stirring well. Combine flour and next 4 ingredients. Add to sugar mixture; stir well.

Pour batter into an 8-inch square pan coated with cooking spray. Bake at 350° for 22 minutes or until a wooden pick inserted in center comes out clean. Sprinkle with marshmallows; bake 1 additional minute or until marshmallows melt. Sprinkle with chocolate. Cool completely. Cut into squares. Yield: 16 brownies.

PER BROWNIE: 100 CALORIES (28% FROM FAT)
FAT 3.1G (SATURATED FAT 0.9G)
PROTEIN 1.6G CARBOHYDRATE 17.2G
CHOLESTEROL 0MG SODIUM 53MG

DOUBLE-CHOCOLATE CHEWS

(pictured on page 131)

1¾ cups all-purpose flour
2¼ teaspoons baking powder
⅛ teaspoon salt
⅔ cup sifted powdered sugar
⅓ cup unsweetened cocoa
1 cup semisweet chocolate mini-morsels, divided
3 tablespoons vegetable oil
1 cup firmly packed brown sugar
2½ tablespoons light-colored corn syrup
1 tablespoon water
2½ teaspoons vanilla extract
3 egg whites, lightly beaten
Vegetable cooking spray

Combine first 5 ingredients; stir well. Set aside. Combine ¾ cup mini-morsels and oil in a small saucepan; cook over low heat, stirring constantly, until chocolate melts. Pour into a large bowl, and cool 5 minutes. Add brown sugar and next 4 ingredients to chocolate mixture; stir well. Stir in flour mixture and remaining ¼ cup mini-morsels.

Drop dough by level tablespoons 2 inches apart onto cookie sheets coated with cooking spray. Bake at 350° for 8 minutes. Cool 2 minutes. Remove cookies to wire racks to cool. Yield: 4 dozen.

PER COOKIE: 64 CALORIES (23% FROM FAT)
FAT 1.6G (SATURATED FAT 0.6G)
PROTEIN 0.9G CARBOHYDRATE 11.8G
CHOLESTEROL 0MG SODIUM 13MG

Baking Better Cookies

• When a recipe calls for softened margarine, the margarine should be just soft enough to blend smoothly with the other ingredients.

• Use regular stick margarine instead of diet margarine or tub margarine.

• Cookie sheets should be at least 2 inches narrower and shorter than the oven rack to allow heat to circulate freely.

• To keep dough from spreading before baking, allow the cookie sheet to cool between batches.

CRISPY OATMEAL COOKIES

½ cup stick margarine, softened
½ cup sugar
½ cup firmly packed brown sugar
½ cup fat-free egg substitute
1 teaspoon vanilla extract
1½ cups all-purpose flour
1 teaspoon baking powder
¾ teaspoon baking soda
¼ teaspoon salt
1¾ cups quick-cooking oats, uncooked
1½ cups corn flakes cereal
Vegetable cooking spray

Beat margarine in a large bowl at medium speed of an electric mixture until creamy; gradually add sugars, beating until light and fluffy. Add egg substitute and vanilla; beat well.

Combine flour and next 3 ingredients, stirring well. Add flour mixture to margarine mixture, mixing well. Stir in oats and cereal.

Drop dough by level tablespoons, 2 inches apart, onto cookie sheets coated with cooking spray. Bake at 350° for 12 to 14 minutes. Remove from cookie sheets, and cool completely on wire racks. Yield: 4 dozen.

PER COOKIE: 63 CALORIES (31% FROM FAT)
FAT 2.2G (SATURATED FAT 0.4G)
PROTEIN 1.2G   CARBOHYDRATE 9.7G
CHOLESTEROL 0MG   SODIUM 67MG

EASY PEANUT BUTTER COOKIES

1⅔ cups all-purpose flour
1¾ teaspoons baking powder
½ teaspoon baking soda
1½ tablespoons cornstarch
¾ cup firmly packed brown sugar
¼ cup vegetable oil
¼ cup sugar
¼ cup creamy peanut butter
1½ tablespoons light-colored corn syrup
2½ teaspoons vanilla extract
1 egg
Vegetable cooking spray
3 tablespoons sugar

Combine first 4 ingredients; stir well. Set aside.

Combine brown sugar and next 3 ingredients in a large bowl; beat at medium speed of an electric mixer until well blended. Add syrup, vanilla, and egg; beat well. Stir in flour mixture.

Coat hands lightly with cooking spray, and shape dough into 48 (1-inch) balls. Roll balls in 3 tablespoons sugar; place 2 inches apart on cookie sheets coated with cooking spray. Flatten balls with the bottom of a glass.

Bake cookies at 375° for 7 minutes or until lightly browned. Remove from cookie sheets; cool on wire racks. Yield: 4 dozen.

PER COOKIE: 59 CALORIES (31% FROM FAT)
FAT 2.0G (SATURATED FAT 0.4G)
PROTEIN 1.0G   CARBOHYDRATE 9.5G
CHOLESTEROL 5MG   SODIUM 23MG

Easy Peanut Butter Cookies and Double-Chocolate Chews (recipe on page 129)

MOLASSES CRACKLES

2⅔ cups all-purpose flour
1¼ teaspoons baking powder
¼ teaspoon baking soda
⅛ teaspoon salt
2¼ teaspoons ground cinnamon
1 teaspoon ground ginger
¾ teaspoon ground cloves
½ cup dark molasses
¼ cup plus 3 tablespoons vegetable oil
2½ tablespoons dark corn syrup
¼ teaspoon grated orange rind
1⅓ cups sifted powdered sugar, divided
1 egg
Vegetable cooking spray

Combine first 7 ingredients; stir well. Set aside.

Combine molasses and next 3 ingredients in a large bowl; beat at medium speed of an electric mixer until blended. Add 1 cup powdered sugar and egg; beat until well blended. Stir flour mixture into molasses mixture. Cover and freeze 1 hour.

Coat hands lightly with cooking spray, and shape dough into 48 (1-inch) balls. Roll balls in remaining ⅓ cup powdered sugar; place 2 inches apart on cookie sheets coated with cooking spray. Bake at 375° for 8 minutes. Cool 2 minutes or until firm. Remove from cookie sheets; cool on wire racks. Yield: 4 dozen.

PER COOKIE: 69 CALORIES (29% FROM FAT)
FAT 2.2G (SATURATED FAT 0.4G)
PROTEIN 0.9G CARBOHYDRATE 11.7G
CHOLESTEROL 5MG SODIUM 17MG

EASY PEACH COBBLER

A low-fat dough flavored with peach syrup bakes up around peach slices for a healthy peach cobbler.

Vegetable cooking spray
¼ cup reduced-calorie stick margarine, melted
2 (16-ounce) cans sliced peaches in light syrup, undrained
¾ cup all-purpose flour
1 teaspoon baking powder
½ cup plus 2 tablespoons sugar
¼ cup skim milk

Coat a 9-inch square baking dish with cooking spray. Pour margarine into dish. Set aside.

Drain peaches, reserving ½ cup syrup. Set peaches aside.

Combine flour, baking powder, and sugar in a medium bowl. Add reserved ½ cup peach syrup and milk, stirring well. Pour batter evenly over margarine. Spoon peaches over batter. (Do not stir.) Bake, uncovered, at 375° for 35 to 40 minutes or until golden. Yield: 6 servings.

PER SERVING: 244 CALORIES (19% FROM FAT)
FAT 5.2G (SATURATED FAT 0.7G)
PROTEIN 2.5G CARBOHYDRATE 50.0G
CHOLESTEROL 0MG SODIUM 85MG

Quick Desserts

• Make a parfait by layering orange sherbet, gingersnap crumbs, mandarin orange segments, and toasted coconut in a tall glass.

• Sprinkle cinnamon-sugar over apple wedges, and microwave at HIGH.

• Freeze peeled ripe bananas, and puree them in a food processor.

• Swirl peanut butter into softened vanilla nonfat frozen yogurt; sprinkle with chocolate cookie crumbs.

• Process canned undrained mixed fruit in a food processor until smooth. Freeze in a shallow pan; return to processor, and process until the consistency of sherbet.

Easy Peach Cobbler

LEMON CREAM PIE
(pictured on page 122)

1 cup low-fat cinnamon graham cracker
   crumbs (about 7 crackers)
¼ cup reduced-calorie stick margarine, melted
¾ cup sugar
¼ cup plus 3 tablespoons cornstarch
⅛ teaspoon salt
1 cup water
⅔ cup nonfat buttermilk
½ cup fat-free egg substitute
2 teaspoons grated lemon rind
½ cup fresh lemon juice
2½ cups frozen reduced-calorie whipped
   topping, thawed
Lemon zest (optional)
Lemon rind curls (optional)
Fresh mint sprigs (optional)

Combine cracker crumbs and margarine; stir well.
Press onto bottom and up sides of a 9-inch pieplate. Bake at 350° for 8 to 10 minutes or until
golden. Remove from oven; cool on a wire rack.

Combine sugar, cornstarch, and salt in a saucepan; gradually stir in water and buttermilk. Cook
over medium heat, stirring constantly, until mixture
comes to a boil. Cook, stirring constantly, 1 minute.

Gradually stir about one-fourth of hot mixture
into egg substitute; add egg substitute mixture to
remaining hot mixture, stirring constantly. Cook
over medium heat, stirring constantly, 2 minutes or
until thickened. Remove from heat; stir in 2 teaspoons lemon rind and lemon juice.

Spoon lemon filling into prepared crust. Cover
and chill at least 2 hours. Spread whipped topping
over filling just before serving. If desired, garnish
with lemon zest, lemon rind curls, and fresh mint
sprigs. Yield: 8 servings.

PER SERVING: 251 CALORIES (26% FROM FAT)
FAT 7.2G (SATURATED FAT 2.6G)
PROTEIN 4.1G CARBOHYDRATE 46.4G
CHOLESTEROL 1MG SODIUM 175MG

FROZEN PEANUT BUTTER PIE

½ cup graham cracker crumbs
2 tablespoons honey
Vegetable cooking spray
¾ cup nonfat ricotta cheese
½ cup tub-style nonfat cream cheese
½ cup sifted powdered sugar
¼ cup chunky peanut butter
½ teaspoon vanilla extract
1 cup frozen reduced-calorie whipped topping,
   thawed
1 cup sliced ripe banana
½ (1-ounce) square semisweet chocolate

Combine crumbs and honey; stir well. Press onto
bottom and 1 inch up sides of a 9-inch pieplate
coated with cooking spray. Bake at 350° for 5 minutes. Cool on a wire rack.

Combine cheeses in a bowl; beat at high speed of
an electric mixer 1½ minutes. Add powdered sugar,
peanut butter, and vanilla; beat at high speed 45
seconds or until well blended. Gently fold whipped
topping into peanut butter mixture.

Arrange banana over crust. Pour peanut butter
filling over banana; set aside.

Place chocolate in a heavy-duty, zip-top plastic
bag, and seal bag. Submerge bag in boiling water
until chocolate melts. Snip off a tiny corner of bag;
drizzle chocolate over pie. Cover and freeze at least
3 hours. Let stand at room temperature 15 minutes
before serving. Yield: 8 servings.

PER SERVING: 190 CALORIES (26% FROM FAT)
FAT 5.4G (SATURATED FAT 1.2G)
PROTEIN 7.9G CARBOHYDRATE 27.3G
CHOLESTEROL 5MG SODIUM 174MG

Frozen Peanut Butter Pie

OLD-FASHIONED BANANA PUDDING

Use bananas that are ripe but firm; they will be sweeter and more flavorful.

⅓ cup all-purpose flour
Dash of salt
2½ cups 1% low-fat milk
1 (14-ounce) can fat-free sweetened condensed milk
2 large egg yolks
2 teaspoons vanilla extract
3 cups sliced ripe banana, divided
45 reduced-fat vanilla wafers, divided
4 large egg whites
¼ cup sugar

Combine flour and salt in a medium saucepan. Gradually add milks and yolks; stir well. Cook over medium heat, stirring constantly, 8 minutes or until thickened. Remove from heat; stir in vanilla.

Arrange 1 cup banana slices in a 2-quart baking dish. Spoon one-third of pudding mixture over banana. Arrange 15 wafers over pudding. Repeat layers twice, arranging last 15 wafers around edge of dish. Push wafers into pudding.

Beat egg whites at high speed of an electric mixer until foamy. Gradually add sugar, 1 tablespoon at a time, beating until stiff peaks form. Spread meringue evenly over pudding, sealing to edge of dish. Bake at 325° for 25 minutes or until golden. Yield: 10 (¾-cup) servings.

Note: This pudding may be a bit soupy when you first remove it from the oven. To thicken, let it cool at least 30 minutes before serving.

PER SERVING: 255 CALORIES (10% FROM FAT)
FAT 2.9G (SATURATED FAT 1.0G)
PROTEIN 7.9G CARBOHYDRATE 49.5G
CHOLESTEROL 51MG SODIUM 155MG

FAVORITE CHOCOLATE PUDDING

⅔ cup sugar
⅓ cup unsweetened cocoa
¼ cup cornstarch
1 tablespoon all-purpose flour
⅛ teaspoon salt
3 cups 1% low-fat milk
1 tablespoon margarine
1 teaspoon vanilla extract
¼ cup plus 2 tablespoons frozen reduced-calorie whipped topping, thawed

Combine first 5 ingredients in a saucepan; stir well. Gradually add milk, stirring with a wire whisk until well blended. Bring to a boil over medium heat; cook, stirring constantly, 1 minute. Remove from heat; stir in margarine and vanilla.

Spoon ½ cup pudding into each of six individual dessert dishes. Cover with plastic wrap; cool to room temperature. Chill pudding at least 3 hours. Remove plastic wrap; top each serving with 1 tablespoon whipped topping. Yield: 6 (½-cup) servings.

PER SERVING: 211 CALORIES (19% FROM FAT)
FAT 4.4G (SATURATED FAT 1.9G)
PROTEIN 5.7G CARBOHYDRATE 37.4G
CHOLESTEROL 5MG SODIUM 138MG

CREAMY RICE PUDDING

1 cup 2% low-fat milk
2 egg yolks
½ cup sugar, divided
½ teaspoon ground cinnamon
⅛ teaspoon ground nutmeg
1 teaspoon vanilla extract
3 cups 2% low-fat milk
3 cups cooked long-grain rice (cooked without salt or fat)
¾ cup raisins

Cook 1 cup milk in a heavy saucepan over medium heat to 180° or until tiny bubbles form around edge of pan.

Beat egg yolks in a medium bowl at high speed of an electric mixer until thick and pale (about 5 minutes). Gradually add ¼ cup sugar, and beat mixture 1 minute. Gradually add hot milk, stirring with a wire whisk until well blended.

Pour mixture into a medium saucepan; cook over medium heat, stirring constantly with a wire whisk, until thickened. Remove from heat; stir in cinnamon, nutmeg, and vanilla. Set aside.

Bring 3 cups milk to a boil over medium heat in a large heavy saucepan, stirring often. Reduce heat to medium-low; add rice and remaining ¼ cup sugar. Cook 30 minutes or until milk is absorbed, stirring often. Fold in egg yolk mixture and raisins. Serve warm or chilled. Yield: 12 (½-cup) servings.

Note: To achieve the best consistency, use regular long-grain (not converted) rice.

PER SERVING: 166 CALORIES (14% FROM FAT)
FAT 2.5G (SATURATED FAT 1.3G)
PROTEIN 4.5G CARBOHYDRATE 31.6G
CHOLESTEROL 43MG SODIUM 43MG

AMBROSIA COMPOTE

1 (15¼-ounce) can pineapple chunks in juice, undrained
¼ cup sugar
¼ cup unsweetened apple juice
1 tablespoon lime juice
¼ teaspoon coconut extract
1½ cups orange sections (about 2 large)
1 cup sliced banana (about 1 large)
1 quart raspberry sherbet
1 (10-ounce) bottle club soda, chilled

Drain pineapple, reserving ¼ cup juice. Combine reserved juice, sugar, and next 3 ingredients; stir until sugar dissolves.

Combine pineapple, orange, and banana in a medium bowl; pour juice mixture over fruit. Cover and chill at least 4 hours. To serve, spoon fruit mixture evenly into individual dessert bowls, using a slotted spoon. Top each serving with ½ cup sherbet and 2½ tablespoons club soda. Serve immediately. Yield: 8 servings.

PER SERVING: 199 CALORIES (5% FROM FAT)
FAT 1.0G (SATURATED FAT 0.0G)
PROTEIN 1.5G CARBOHYDRATE 47.7G
CHOLESTEROL 0MG SODIUM 75MG

Creamy Rice Pudding

Banana Boat

BANANA BOATS

4 small firm bananas, peeled and split
   lengthwise
1 tablespoon lemon juice
1 cup vanilla nonfat frozen yogurt
1 cup strawberry nonfat frozen yogurt
¼ cup chocolate syrup
1 tablespoon plus 1 teaspoon finely chopped
   pecans

  Place 2 banana halves into each of four individual
dessert dishes. Brush banana halves with lemon

juice. Scoop ¼ cup vanilla yogurt and ¼ cup strawberry yogurt over banana halves in each dish.
  Top each serving with 1 tablespoon syrup and 1
teaspoon chopped pecans. Serve immediately.
Yield: 4 servings.

PER SERVING: 251 CALORIES (9% FROM FAT)
FAT 2.5G (SATURATED FAT 0.4G)
PROTEIN 5.2G   CARBOHYDRATE 56.2G
CHOLESTEROL 0MG   SODIUM 70MG

BANANA SPLIT ICE CREAM

4 egg yolks, lightly beaten
5 cups 1% low-fat milk, divided
2 (14-ounce) cans fat-free sweetened
   condensed skim milk
2 cups mashed ripe banana
2 tablespoons fresh lime juice
2 tablespoons vanilla extract
¾ cup fat-free double-chocolate sundae syrup
½ cup chopped pecans, toasted
⅓ cup maraschino cherries, quartered

Combine egg yolks and 2½ cups 1% low-fat milk in a medium-size heavy saucepan; stir well with a wire whisk. Cook over medium heat, stirring constantly, 10 minutes or until mixture thickens and will coat a spoon (do not boil). Combine egg yolk mixture, remaining 2½ cups 1% low-fat milk, and condensed milk in a large bowl; stir well. Cover and chill thoroughly.

Add banana, lime juice, and vanilla to milk mixture; stir well. Pour mixture into freezer container of a 1-gallon hand-turned or electric freezer. Freeze according to manufacturer's instructions. Spoon ice cream into a large freezer-safe container; fold in syrup, pecans, and cherries. Cover and freeze 2 hours or until firm. Yield: 24 (½-cup) servings.

PER SERVING: 189 CALORIES (15% FROM FAT)
FAT 3.2G (SATURATED FAT 0.8G)
PROTEIN 5.3G   CARBOHYDRATE 34.3G
CHOLESTEROL 40MG   SODIUM 67MG

MILK AND COOKIES ICE CREAM

2 cups 1% low-fat milk
1 cup evaporated skimmed milk
⅔ cup sugar
½ cup fat-free egg substitute
1 teaspoon vanilla extract
1 cup coarsely crushed chocolate wafers
   (about 3 ounces)

Combine first 5 ingredients in a bowl; beat at medium speed of an electric mixer until well blended.

Pour milk mixture into freezer container of a 2-quart hand-turned or electric freezer. Freeze according to manufacturer's instructions. Spoon into a freezer-safe container; stir in crushed chocolate wafers. Cover and freeze at least 1 hour before serving. Yield: 10 (½-cup) servings.

PER SERVING: 130 CALORIES (14% FROM FAT)
FAT 2.0G (SATURATED FAT 0.7G)
PROTEIN 5.2G   CARBOHYDRATE 22.8G
CHOLESTEROL 8MG   SODIUM 98MG

CARAMEL-APPLE SAUCE

½ cup low-fat sweetened condensed milk
½ cup coarsely chopped Rome apple
¼ cup unsweetened apple juice
3 tablespoons brown sugar
1 teaspoon vanilla extract

Pour milk into a 1-quart casserole dish. Cover and place in a large shallow pan. Add hot water to pan to depth of ¼ inch. Bake at 425° for 1 hour or until condensed milk is thick and caramel colored (add hot water to pan as needed). Remove from oven; uncover and cool.

Combine apple, apple juice, and sugar in a medium saucepan. Bring to a boil; cover, reduce heat, and simmer 2 minutes or until apple is tender. Add caramelized milk and vanilla to apple mixture; stir well. Cook, stirring constantly, until thoroughly heated. Serve warm over fat-free pound cake or vanilla nonfat ice cream. Yield: 1 cup.

PER TABLESPOON: 44 CALORIES (8% FROM FAT)
FAT 0.4G (SATURATED FAT 0.3G)
PROTEIN 0.8G   CARBOHYDRATE 9.3G
CHOLESTEROL 1MG   SODIUM 11MG

CHUNKY PINEAPPLE SAUCE

2 tablespoons margarine
3 cups coarsely chopped fresh pineapple
¾ cup firmly packed brown sugar
2 tablespoons cornstarch
1⅓ cups unsweetened pineapple juice
1 tablespoon light rum (optional)

Heat margarine in a large skillet over medium-high heat until melted. Add chopped pineapple, and sauté 4 to 5 minutes or until pineapple is tender.

Combine sugar and cornstarch. Gradually stir in pineapple juice. Pour over pineapple mixture. Cook over medium heat, stirring constantly, until thickened and bubbly. Remove from heat. Stir in rum, if desired. Serve over angel food cake, fat-free pound cake, or nonfat ice cream; top with reduced-calorie whipped topping, if desired. Yield: 3½ cups.

PER TABLESPOON: 24 CALORIES (15% FROM FAT)
FAT 0.4G (SATURATED FAT 0.1G)
PROTEIN 0.1G CARBOHYDRATE 5.1G
CHOLESTEROL 0MG SODIUM 6MG

Chunky Pineapple Sauce

INDEX

METRIC EQUIVALENTS

Metric Equivalents for Different Types of Ingredients

A standard cup measure of a dry or solid ingredient will vary in weight depending on the type of ingredient. A standard cup of liquid is the same volume for any type of liquid. Use the following chart when converting standard cup measures to grams (weight) or milliliters (volume).

Standard Cup	Fine Powder (ex. flour)	Grain (ex. rice)	Granular (ex. sugar)	Liquid Solids (ex. butter)	Liquid (ex. milk)
1	140 g	150 g	190 g	200 g	240 ml
¾	105 g	113 g	143 g	150 g	180 ml
⅔	93 g	100 g	125 g	133 g	160 ml
½	70 g	75 g	95 g	100 g	120 ml
⅓	47 g	50 g	63 g	67 g	80 ml
¼	35 g	38 g	48 g	50 g	60 ml
⅛	18 g	19 g	24 g	25 g	30 ml

Useful Equivalents for Liquid Ingredients by Volume

¼ tsp					=	1 ml	
½ tsp					=	2 ml	
1 tsp					=	5 ml	
3 tsp	=	1 tbls		= ½ fl oz	=	15 ml	
		2 tbls	= ⅛ cup	= 1 fl oz	=	30 ml	
		4 tbls	= ¼ cup	= 2 fl oz	=	60 ml	
		5⅓ tbls	= ⅓ cup	= 3 fl oz	=	80 ml	
		8 tbls	= ½ cup	= 4 fl oz	=	120 ml	
		10⅔ tbls	= ⅔ cup	= 5 fl oz	=	160 ml	
		12 tbls	= ¾ cup	= 6 fl oz	=	180 ml	
		16 tbls	= 1 cup	= 8 fl oz	=	240 ml	
		1 pt	= 2 cups	= 16 fl oz	=	480 ml	
		1 qt	= 4 cups	= 32 fl oz	=	960 ml	
				33 fl oz	=	1000 ml	= 1 l

Useful Equivalents for Dry Ingredients by Weight

(To convert ounces to grams, multiply the number of ounces by 30.)

1 oz	=	¹⁄₁₆ lb	=	30 g
4 oz	=	¼ lb	=	120 g
8 oz	=	½ lb	=	240 g
12 oz	=	¾ lb	=	360 g
16 oz	=	1 lb	=	480 g

Useful Equivalents for Cooking/Oven Temperatures

	Fahrenheit	Celcius	Gas Mark
Freeze Water	32° F	0° C	
Room Temperature	68° F	20° C	
Boil Water	212° F	100° C	
Bake	325° F	160° C	3
	350° F	180° C	4
	375° F	190° C	5
	400° F	200° C	6
	425° F	220° C	7
	450° F	230° C	8
Broil			Grill

Useful Equivalents for Length

(To convert inches to centimeters, multiply the number of inches by 2.5.)

1 in				=	2.5 cm		
6 in	=	½ ft		=	15 cm		
12 in	=	1 ft		=	30 cm		
36 in	=	3 ft	= 1 yd	=	90 cm		
40 in				=	100 cm	=	1 m